THE 100+ SERIES™

Reproducible Activities

Using the Standards

Building Grammar & Writing Skills

Grade 4

By
Anne L. Steele

Published by Instructional Fair
an imprint of
Frank Schaffer Publications®

Instructional Fair

Author: Anne L. Steele

Editors: Stephanie Oberc, Christine Hood, Marsha Elyn Wright

Frank Schaffer Publications®

Instructional Fair is an imprint of Frank Schaffer Publications.

Send all inquiries to:
Frank Schaffer Publications
3195 Wilson Drive NW
Grand Rapids, Michigan 49544

Using the Standards: Building Grammar & Writing Skills—grade 4

ISBN: 0-7424-1804-9

4 5 6 7 8 9 10 RRDW 09 08 07 06 05

Introduction

The International Reading Association and the National Council of Teachers of English have presented 12 standards for the English Language Arts. This book provides a collection of standards-based reproducibles that aim to focus on grammar and writing. It is part of the 100+ Using the Standards—Building Grammar and Writing Skills series that provides students with opportunities to develop the language skills they need to pursue life's goals and to participate fully as informed, productive members of society.

100+ Using the Standards— Building Grammar and Writing Skills, Grade 4 can be used as supplemental material to reinforce any existing language arts program. This book is divided into five sections: capitalization, punctuation, parts of speech, usage, writing strategies, and writing applications. The activities are designed to expand and strengthen students' literacy abilities learned in previous grades so as to develop proficient written expression. They may be used sequentially as they appear in the book or in random order.

Grammar is a vital part of communication, and writing is a powerful instrument of communication. To help students learn good grammar and to become more effective, expressive writers, basic grammar skills and writing strategies and activities should be an essential component in every student's educational experience.

This book contains the necessary skills each fourth-grade student should learn in order to develop good grammar. We recommend that you use these grammar exercises to introduce students to the particular skill, and then have students focus on this skill in their own writing. For example, if the skill is possessives, have students focus on checking for proper use of apostrophes during the revision and editing stages of their writing.

The writing strategies section provides various tips to use during each step of the writing process. It begins with organization and focus activities, such as determining the audience and purpose and learning how to effectively organize a paragraph or multi-paragraph essay. There are also activities using various reference materials, as well as editing and revision techniques to help students develop a coherent, unified paragraph or multi-paragraph essay.

The writing applications section has students write in a variety of genres from fairy tales to biographies to poetry. The activities cover a variety of forms (letters, essays, stories, and reviews) for a variety of purposes (to inform, persuade, describe) and for a variety of audiences (other students, principals, authors). Each form, purpose, and audience demands differences in style, tone, approach, and choice of words. A wide variety of writing experiences is critical to developing effective writing.

Please keep in mind that perfection in mechanics and writing skills develop over time. This book is a tool to use in helping students build upon their knowledge and become proficient in the English language.

0-7424-1804-9 *Building Grammar & Writing Skills*

English Language Arts Standards

1. Read a wide range of texts.

2. Read a wide range of literature.

3. Apply a variety of strategies to comprehend and interpret texts.

4. Use spoken, written, and visual language to communicate effectively.

5. Use a variety of strategies while writing and use elements of the writing process to communicate.

6. Apply knowledge of language structure and conventions, media techniques, figurative language, and genre to create, critique, and discuss texts.

7. Research issues and interests, pose questions, and gather data to communicate discoveries.

8. Work with a variety of technological and other resources to collect information and to communicate knowledge.

9. Understand and respect the differences in language use across cultures, regions, and social roles.

10. Students whose first language is not English use their first language to develop competencies in English and other content areas.

11. Participate in a variety of literary communities.

12. Use spoken, written, and visual language to accomplish purposes.

Published by Instructional Fair. Copyright protected. 0-7424-1804-9 *Building Grammar & Writing Skills*

Table of Contents	Standards Reflected	Page
Introduction		3
Grammar: Capitalization		
Rollicking Riddles	4, 6	9
A Little Respect	4, 6	10
Capital Chaos	4, 6	11
Around the World	4, 6	12
Silly Scramble	4, 6	13
Our Multilingual Nation	4, 6	14
Tricky Titles	4, 6	15
Camp Cayuga	4, 6	16
Crazy Quotes	4, 6	17
Grammar: Punctuation		
Abbreviation Match-up	4, 6	18
Perfect Punctuation	4, 6	19
Thank-You Letters	4, 6	20
Tongue Twisters	4, 6	21
Comma Cleanup	4, 6	22
Meet the Authors	4, 6	23
Cool Commas	4, 6	24
What Do You Say?	4, 6	25
Short Titles	4, 6	26
Titles Galore	4, 6	27
Pick the Possessive	4, 6	28
Marco Polo	4, 6	29
Grammar: Parts of Speech		
Parts of Speech Puzzle	4, 6	30
Recipe for Plurals	4, 6	31
Possessives Sort	4, 6	32
Birthday Party	4, 6	33
Pronoun Power	4, 6	34
It's a Cover-up	4, 6	35
In the Past	4, 6	36
Go Fish! Verbs Game	4, 6	37
A Little Help	4, 6	38
A Tall Tale	4, 6	39
Lots of Links	4, 6	40
Describing Details	4, 6	41

Published by Instructional Fair. Copyright protected.

0-7424-1804-9 *Building Grammar & Writing Skills*

Table of Contents	Standards Reflected	Page

Published by Instructional Fair. Copyright protected. 0-7424-1804-9 *Building Grammar & Writing Skills*

Table of Contents	Standards Reflected	Page

Writing Applications: Nonfiction

Writing Applications: Fiction

Published by Instructional Fair. Copyright protected.　　　　　0-7424-1804-9 *Building Grammar & Writing Skills*

Table of Contents	**Standards Reflected**	**Page**

Published by Instructional Fair. Copyright protected.

0-7424-1804-9 *Building Grammar & Writing Skills*

Name _____ Date _____

Rollicking Riddles

Capitalize the names of particular people, animals, places, and things.

Example: **E**mily and her cat, **F**luffy, visited the **W**ashington **M**onument.

Capitalize words like *father*, *mom*, *uncle*, and *aunt* when they are parts of titles or used as proper nouns. Do not capitalize these words when they are common nouns.

Examples: **U**ncle **R**alph rides his bicycle to school.
My mom is swimming.

Circle each word that should begin with a capital letter. Write the first letter of each circled word to answer the riddles.

1. My sister, irene thompson, lives on white avenue. She went to seattle to visit aunt diane and Uncle rob for the weekend. They went to the Seattle aquarium and saw gina, the sea otter, and oscar, the octopus. Next, they ate lunch at neptune Café. father drove the lexus to pick her up at yeager Airport.

Riddle: Why was the knight afraid of the insect? _____

2. My grandmother went to college at The art Institute, while Grandpa jones worked at the indianapolis Zoo. After graduating, grandma became the art teacher at south academy High School. She purchases the art supplies from winchel's Art Center.

Riddle: What kind of saw dances? _____

3. aunt carolyn took oliver to Lake michigan during summer vacation. Over spring break, she will take him to New York to see the Empire State building.

Riddle: What has teeth but can't eat? _____

9

Name _____ Date _____

A Little Respect

Capitalize titles of respect. If the title is abbreviated, it is followed by a period.
Example: I asked **Professor** Smith a question.

Capitalize the personal pronoun *I*.
Example: **I** like ice cream.

Write a different title under each person, such as *Mr.*, *Miss*, or *Professor*.

1.  **2.**  **3.**  **4.**

_____ Garcia   _____ Pham   _____ Yochim   _____ Lowe

Underline three times the letters that should be capitalized.

5. Is mr. daniels your math teacher this year?

6. My brother and i have an appointment with dr. williams.

7. i wrote a letter to senator Marie harrison.

8. miss stanley, mr. parker, and ms. cao are studying to be doctors.

9. When i grow up, i want to be a judge.

10. Will professor pinedo be teaching English next year?

11. When will sergeant davis and captain riley be coming to school to speak?

12. mr. Bernard and i would like to speak with judge yoshi.

0-7424-1804-9 *Building Grammar & Writing Skills*

Name _____ Date _____

Capital Chaos

Help Ozzie correct his capitalization errors by drawing a diagonal line (/) through each letter that should be lowercase. Write the words correctly on the lines.

Use these capitalization tips to help you find all 22 errors.
- Capitalize the names of particular people, animals, places, and things— **C**aptain **M**artinez, **S**pot, **G**alleria **M**all, **C**orvette.
- Do not capitalize common nouns—**c**hild, **t**iger, **b**each, **r**eading, **f**ootball.

_____
_____
_____
_____
_____
_____
_____
_____
_____
_____
_____
_____
_____
_____
_____

My Family and I went to Southern California for summer vacation. We rented a blue Car and stayed at my Aunt and Uncle's house on the Beach. In the morning, my Sister and I would ride our Bikes, while my Father jogged along the Pathway. We saw Dolphins swimming in the Ocean and leaping out of the water! We built Sandcastles, played Volleyball, and went bodysurfing in the Pacific Ocean. We also went to Disneyland and stayed overnight at a Hotel that had the biggest Swimming pool I have ever seen! Another day, we went to the La Brea Tar Pits and saw skeletons of Mammoths, Saber-toothed cats, and giant ground sloths. Our Mom let us buy souvenirs from the Gift shop. I bought a book about fossils, and my Sister Sara bought a sloth puppet. When it was time to go home, Uncle Henry drove us to the Airport. It was an awesome Vacation!

11

Name _____ Date _____

Around the World

Houston
Texas
United States

Begin names of cities, states, and countries with a capital letter.

Begin names of sections of the country or world with a capital letter—the **N**orth, **S**outh **A**merica, the **F**ar **E**ast.

Do not capitalize *north*, *south*, *east* and *west* when they refer to a direction—Drive **east** two miles.

Rewrite these place names in the chart correctly.

paris, france	
montreal, canada	
perth, australia	
denver, colorado	
la paz, mexico	
ankara, turkey	
beijing, china	
nairobi, kenya	

Circle each word that should begin with a capital letter.

1. Costa rica is a small country in central america.

2. Four continents, Europe, africa, Asia, and australia, are in the eastern Hemisphere.

3. Canada is north of the united states.

4. Arizona is in the west, and illinois is in the midwest.

5. China, japan, and hong kong are countries of east Asia.

6. San jose, california is at the southern end of san francisco Bay.

0-7424-1804-9 *Building Grammar & Writing Skills*

Name _____ Date _____

Silly Scramble

Capitalize weekdays, months, and holidays—**W**ednesday, **J**anuary, **L**abor **D**ay. Do not capitalize seasons—**w**inter, **s**pring, **s**ummer, **a**utumn.

Unscramble the boldfaced words. Remember to use capital letters when appropriate.

1. The day before Monday is **nsydua**. _____

2. In **bneevrom**, many people in the United States celebrate **hnsvitakgnig**.
   _____   _____

3. The season between winter and summer is **gpnisr**. _____

4. Hanukkah, Kwanzaa, and **sscathirm** are all celebrated in **emcdreeb**.
   _____   _____

5. On **yma** 5, Cinco de **aymo** is celebrated with parades and parties.
   _____   _____

6. Leaves change color and days become cooler in **utmnua**. _____

7. On the last **nmoady** in May, many Americans observe **lairomem ayd** in memory of those who died while serving in United States wars.
   _____   _____

8. In the Northern Hemisphere, **trwnie** begins on December 21 or 22.
   _____

9. The day after Tuesday is **nesdewyda**. _____

10. Bastille Day, a French national holiday celebrated on **ljyu** 14, marks the capture of the Bastille during the French Revolution. _____

11. The warmest season of the year is **eumsmr**. _____

12. On the second Monday in October, Americans celebrate **uousblcm ayd** to honor Christopher Columbus' voyage to America in 1492.

   _____ _____

13

Name _____ Date _____

Our Multilingual Nation

Capitalize nationalities—**F**rench soldiers, **C**hinese food.
Capitalize all languages—I am taking language classes in **S**panish and **G**erman.
Use the code below to write the missing words. Use capital letters when appropriate.

A	B	C	D	E	F	G	H	I	J	K	L	M
1	2	3	4	5	6	7	8	9	10	11	12	13

N	O	P	Q	R	S	T	U	V	W	X	Y	Z
14	15	16	17	18	19	20	21	22	23	24	25	26

The United States population consists of people of many nationalities and

ethnic groups. My own neighborhood is very diverse. My neighbors are Chinese,

☐☐☐☐☐☐☐☐ , Lebanese, ☐☐☐☐☐☐☐ and ☐☐☐☐☐☐☐ .
 8 9 19 16 1 14 9 3   9 20 1 12 9 1 14   6 18 5 14 3 8

Mr. and Mrs. Phan, who live across the street, speak ☐☐☐☐☐☐☐☐ .
                                                      13 1 14 4 1 18 9 14

Did you know there are different kinds of ☐☐☐☐☐☐ ? There is
                                          3 8 9 14 5 19 5

☐☐☐☐☐☐☐☐☐ , Mandarin, and ☐☐ . Mandarin is the most commonly
 3 1 14 20 15 14 5 19 5   23 21

spoken language in the world! My best friend George is ☐☐☐☐☐☐☐☐ .
                                                        6 9 12 9 16 9 14 15

His family speaks ☐☐☐☐☐☐☐ in their home. Did you know that many
                   20 1 7 1 12 15 7

families speak other languages besides ☐☐☐☐☐☐☐ in their homes?
                                        5 14 7 12 9 19 8

☐☐☐☐☐☐☐ is the second most commonly spoken language in the United
 19 16 1 14 9 19 8

States, and more than one million people also speak French, ☐☐☐☐☐☐ ,
                                                             7 5 18 13 1 14

Italian, and Chinese. My friend Sam's grandfather is a Navajo Indian. He told us

that ☐☐☐☐☐☐ is one of the oldest spoken languages in our country.
      14 1 22 1 10 15

I can speak English and Spanish, but I would like to learn another language, maybe

Mandarin or perhaps ☐☐☐☐☐☐ .
                     8 5 2 18 5 23

14

0-7424-1804-9 *Building Grammar & Writing Skills*

Name _____ Date _____

Tricky Titles

Capitalize the first word, last word, and every other important word in a title.

Do not capitalize short prepositions (*at, by, for, in, of, to, with*), short conjunctions (*and, but, or*), or articles (*a, an, the*), unless they are the first word in a title.

Example: The **B**oy **W**ho **O**wned the **S**chool

Write these book titles correctly.

1. harry potter and the chamber of secrets _____

2. coyotes in the crosswalk _____

3. amber brown is not a crayon _____

Write the newspaper article titles correctly.

4. kermit takes the walk _____

5. red wings win in overtime _____

6. mario and britney play for tennis fans _____

Write the titles of Pablo Picasso's works of art correctly.

7. old woman _____

8. the old guitarist _____

9. young bather with sand shovel _____

10. Write the title of your favorite song. _____

11. Write the title of your favorite movie. _____

12. Write the title of your favorite book. _____

0-7424-1804-9 *Building Grammar & Writing Skills*

Name _____ Date _____

Camp Cayuga

In a friendly letter, capitalize:
- Date
- First word in the greeting—**D**ear Michael
- First word in the closing—**Y**our friend
- First word in each sentence
- Special names of people, places, or things
- Personal pronoun *I*

Read this letter. There are 34 words that should begin with a capital letter. Underline three times the first letter in those words.

august 3, 2002

dear sonja,

    I hope you are having a nice summer. i am at camp cayuga, which is located in the pocono mountains of northeast pennsylvania. I am staying in a cabin with nine other girls. I am having a blast!

    There are so many things to do. they have horseback riding, arts and crafts, kayaking, windsurfing, and water polo. you can also play soccer, softball, tennis, or basketball.

    We also get to go on several field trips. On saturday, we went backpacking on the appalachian trail. Tina slipped and fell during the hike. My counselor, sandy, had to bandage tina's knee. We also took a field trip to dorney park and wild kingdom. They have the tallest wooden roller coaster in the world, hercules. I rode hercules five times in a row. It was so much fun! Next Friday, we are taking another field trip to hershey's chocolate world and amusement park. we get to take a tour of the hershey chocolate Factory to see how chocolate is made. I hope they give free samples, because i love chocolate!

    What have you been doing this summer? Write when you get a chance.

        your friend,
        maria

0-7424-1804-9 *Building Grammar & Writing Skills*

Name _____ Date _____

Crazy Quotes

Direct quotations are the exact words someone says.

Capitalize the first word of the quotation.

Examples: Kim asked, "**W**hat time is it?"
"**F**ive o'clock," Peter replied.

Write *Yes* if the quotation is capitalized correctly. Write *No* if the quotation is not capitalized correctly.

_____ **1.** "It's joke time," said Roberto, the camp counselor. "Does anyone have a joke?"

_____ **2.** "I do, I do!" shouted Shannon.

_____ **3.** "all right, Shannon, tell your joke," said Roberto.

_____ **4.** Shannon asked, "how can you tell that elephants like to swim?"

_____ **5.** "they are always standing in water," answered Samantha.

_____ **6.** "No," said Shannon. "It's because they always have their trunks on."

_____ **7.** "ha, ha, ha," laughed the children.

_____ **8.** Troy called out, "okay, I have joke. What do frogs drink at snack time?"

_____ **9.** "I haven't a clue," responded Chase.

_____ **10.** "Croak-a-Cola," laughed Troy.

_____ **11.** Everyone groaned, "oh, that's bad."

_____ **12.** "we have time for one more joke. Who would like to tell one?"
        asked Roberto.

_____ **13.** "I will," replied Dylan. "where does a cow go on Saturday night?"

_____ **14.** "You've got me," Stacey replied.

_____ **15.** "To the moo-vies," chuckled Dylan.

0-7424-1804-9 *Building Grammar & Writing Skills*

Name _____ Date _____

Abbreviation Match-up

An abbreviation is a short way of writing a word or phrase. An abbreviation usually has a period at the end. If the word begins with a capital letter, its abbreviation should also.

Match each abbreviation to the correct word or words.

a.m.; A.M. •	• December
in. •	• et cetera (and so forth)
etc. •	• Missus
Aug. •	• inches
Blvd. •	• Company
cm •	• August
Dec. •	• ante meridiem (before noon)
E. •	• Doctor
Dr. •	• Boulevard
Mrs. •	• East
Co. •	• centimeter

Feb. •	• October
Jr. •	• Governor
Mt. •	• Junior
Oct. •	• miscellaneous
Mr. •	• January
Gov. •	• Friday
misc. •	• foot; feet
Fri. •	• February
Jan. •	• Mountain; Mount
Gen. •	• Mister
ft. •	• General

kg •	• quart; quarts
ml •	• number
oz. •	• page; pages
qt. •	• kilogram
L •	• pound; pounds
yd. •	• post meridiem (after noon)
lb. •	• ounce; ounces
p.; pp. •	• milliliter
no. •	• yard
p.m.; P.M. •	• liter

W. •	• Reverend
vs.; v. •	• Senior; Sister
Pres. •	• Saint; Street
Sen. •	• West
Rev. •	• Wednesday
Rep. •	• President
St. •	• Senator
Sr. •	• versus
Sept. •	• Representative
Wed. •	• September

0-7424-1804-9 *Building Grammar & Writing Skills*

Name _____ _____ Date _____

Perfect Punctuation

A **declarative sentence** makes a statement. It ends with a period. **(.)**
Example: I am going to the carnival**.**

An **imperative sentence** gives a command. It ends with a period. **(.)**
Example: Please come to the carnival with me**.**

An **interrogative sentence** asks a question. It ends with a question mark. **(?)**
Example: Will you come to the carnival with me**?**

An **exclamatory sentence** shows surprise or great emotion. It ends with an exclamation point. **(!)**
Example: I can't wait to go to the carnival**!**

Write the correct punctuation mark at the end of each sentence.

1. This weekend is the Skateboard Beach Bash in Hermosa Beach
2. Do you want to go on Saturday to watch the Skateboarding Fly Bowl Contest
3. Which skaters will be competing
4. The Young Guns, Jake Brown and Chris Gentry, will be there
5. Count me in
6. Wow, look at the size of that ramp
7. Come on let's find a seat in the stands
8. Who's skating right now
9. It is Jake Brown, and he just spun fives
10. This is going to be a great day
11. Wow, Chris Gentry is unbelievable
12. Did you see that
13. Jake Brown just pulled an awesome double flip mute grab
14. That nollie-to-heelflip-to-f/s, lipslide-to-revert just won for best trick
15. Watching this contest is making me hungry

19

Name _____ Date _____

Thank-You Letters

In a friendly letter and business letter, use a comma:
- To separate the month and day from the year—June 21, 2003
- To separate a city or country from a state—Ottawa Lake, MI
- After the closing—Sincerely,

In a friendly letter, use a comma (,) after the greeting—Dear Mia,

In a business letter, use a colon (:) after the greeting—Dear Mr. Barnes:

Read these letters. Write the missing commas and colons.

July 20 2002
Dear Aunt Marilyn
        Thank you for the beautiful blouse.
Pink is my favorite color. I get compliments
when I wear it.

        Your niece
        Stephanie

March 10 2002

Mr. George Broome
555 West Road
Toledo OH 43617

Dear Mr. Broome

Thank you for coming to speak to our class
during career week. I enjoyed learning about
being a photographer. I especially liked your
photographs of other countries.
I hope you can come back again.
Sincerely yours
Gary Hymes

January 15 2003

Ms. Barbara Foster
879 Vine Street
Anywhere CA 90045

Dear Ms. Foster

Thank you for sending me the information
about the museum. It was very helpful in
writing my report for school.

Sincerely
Trish Rodriquez

December 5 2002

Dear Ricky

        Thank you for the charm
bracelet. It is gorgeous. I wear it all
the time!
                Love
                Jenna

20

Name _____ Date _____

Tongue Twisters

A comma (,) tells the reader to pause. Use a comma to separate three or more words or phrases in a series.

Examples: I ate a banana, cereal, and yogurt for breakfast. (words)
This morning I took a shower, got dressed, and ate breakfast. (phrases)

Read these sentences. Then add the missing commas

1. Wendy Wesley and William are washing Wilma Winkel's windows.

2. Silly Sally sat on a steeple sipping soda sewing shirts and singing spooky songs.

3. Last night, Lannie Lily and Larry licked lollipops while buying lemons licorice and lettuce at Lucky's.

4. Big Bill Boone Bonnie Bell and Barry Burke baked bread while bouncing blue basketballs.

5. Yesterday, handsome Harry hung a hammock played the harmonica and hit a homerun.

6. Jonathan Julie Jacob and Joseph are juggling jugs and jumping rope.

7. Miss Mary Moore makes many mini muffins milks cows and mends mittens.

Write a sentence naming your:

8. Three favorite TV shows

_____

9. Four favorite foods

_____

10. Three things you like to do

_____

0-7424-1804-9 *Building Grammar & Writing Skills*

Name _____ Date _____

Comma Cleanup

A comma (,) tells the reader to pause.

Use a comma to separate the person (or people) addressed from what is said.
Example: Mona, are you going to the beach on Saturday?

Use a comma after introductory words.
Example: Yes, I saw that movie.

Use a comma after an interjection at the beginning of a sentence.
Example: Wow, did you see that flash of lightning?

Read each set of sentences.
Add the missing commas.

1. What is the capital of the United States Nathan?
   Oh that's an easy one. It's Washington, D.C.

2. Class what do the members of Congress do at the United States Capitol?
   Yes Stacey do you know the answer?
   Yes Mr. Davidson Congress makes our nation's laws.

3. Jessica or Joaquin could you explain what is the U.S. Constitution?
   Wow that's a hard one!
   Mr. Davidson I think I know.
   Yes Joaquin. It's a written document that defines the structure and purpose
   of the U.S. government.
   Very good Joaquin.

4. Heather what does the Bill of Rights in the Constitution describe?
   Hmmm let me think a minute. The Bill of Rights describes the basic rights and
   freedoms of all Americans, and forbids the government to violate these rights.
   Excellent job Heather.
   Thank you Mr. Davidson.

22

0-7424-1804-9 *Building Grammar & Writing Skills*

Name _____ Date _____

Meet the Authors

A **comma** (,) tells the reader to pause.
An **appositive** is a word or phrase that explains or identifies a noun.

Use a comma to separate an appositive that immediately
follows a noun from the rest of the sentence.

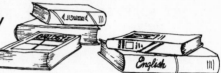

Example: I've read *Fudge-A-Mania,* my favorite book, six times.

Read each sentence. Then add the missing commas.

1. Jerry Spinelli won the 1991 Newbery Medal for *Maniac Magee* the sixth
of his more than 15 acclaimed books for young readers.

2. E.L. Konigsburg the author of *From the Mixed-up Files of Mrs. Basil E.
Frankweiler* grew up in a small mill town in Pennsylvania.

3. *The Hockey Machine* by Matt Christopher is a story about Steve Crandell a
talented hockey player who is kidnapped by a wealthy boy who wants Steve
to play on his hockey team.

4. J.K. Rowling author of the Harry Potter books wrote her first story when she
was five or six years old.

5. In 1969, Judy Blume published her first book *The One in the Middle Is the
Green Kangaroo.*

6. Betsy Duffy got the idea to write *A Boy in the Doghouse* when her family was
housebreaking their dog Chester.

7. Gary Soto an acclaimed poet, essayist, and fiction writer originally wanted to
become a paleontologist a scientist who studies fossils and bones.

8. Paula Danziger a children's author of more than 25 books knew she wanted
to be a writer when she was a child but did not begin writing until almost 30
years later.

23

Name _____ Date _____

Cool Commas

A **compound sentence** is made up of two independent clauses.
Use a **comma** followed by a coordinating conjunction (*and, but, or, for, nor, yet, so*) to combine the independent clauses.

Example: Theresa reads novels. Jessica reads poetry. (but)
Theresa reads novels, **but** Jessica reads poetry.

Use the two independent clauses and the conjunction in parentheses to write a compound sentence. Remember to use a comma before the conjunction.

1. I went to the store. John went to the movies. (and)

_____

2. Mary ran to the car. Bill ran to the bus. (but)

_____

3. It was raining all day. I was dry under my umbrella. (yet)

_____

4. Vanessa ate the pizza. Gillian ate the chocolate cake. (so)

_____

5. The puppy slept. The cat played with a ball of yarn. (and)

_____

6. We played volleyball. The weather was sunny and warm. (for)

_____

7. Kimberly will go to the grocery store. She will not take a nap. (so)

_____

8. Mehrad will play baseball. He will play football. (or)

_____

9. Kangaroos are furry. They have a pocket. (and)

_____

10. Whales live in water. They are not fish. (but)

_____

24

Name _____ Date _____

What Do You Say?

Use quotation marks (" ") to show the exact words a speaker says.
Example: Trey said, "I like mint chocolate chip ice cream."

Use a comma (,) to set off the exact words a speaker says from the rest of
the sentence.

Examples: "Coffee ice cream is my favorite," said Lisa.

Write the missing punctuation marks.

1. Logan asked   May I get a dog for my birthday?

2. No, you're too young to have a dog   Mom replied.

3. But, I am going to be five years old in December   whined Logan.

4. Mom explained   Having a dog is a huge responsibility. You have to feed it, take

   it on walks, and clean up after it.

5. Logan exclaimed   I can do all that! If I get a dog, I promise I'll take care of it.

6. Jacob inquired   What is Logan whining about?

7. He wants a dog for his birthday, but he is too young   explained Mom.

8. Jacob commented   I have always wanted a dog. I'm old enough, aren't I?

9. Mom responded   No, you may not get a dog.

10. But, Mom, I promise to take it on walks every day   Jacob explained.

11. Mom shook her head, smiled and said   No Jacob, we really don't have the room.

12. Logan and Jacob both asked together   Can we get a dog next year

0-7424-1804-9 *Building Grammar & Writing Skills*

Name _____ Date _____

Short Titles

Use quotation marks around titles of short works such as stories, songs, poems, magazine and newspaper articles, and book chapters.

Examples: "Uncle Wiggly Loses His Pants" (short story)
"America the Beautiful" (song)

Use the titles from the box to write a title for each newspaper or magazine article below.

Dangerous Floods in Europe	Gold Coin Rakes in Millions
Justin's Music 101	Spotlight on Kids' Safety

1. The world's most valuable coin is sold for a record $7.6 million!

_____

2. Thousands flee as torrential rains flood many European cities.

_____

3. The president will host a conference to raise awareness about kids' safety.

_____

4. 'N Sync's Justin Timberlake wants music education to be available to all kids.

_____

Write a sentence using each title. Remember to use correct punctuation.

5. Over the Rainbow (song)

_____

6. Three Little Pigs (title of a story)

_____

7. Trumpet Player (poem)

_____

8. The Missing Shoe (chapter of a book)

_____

0-7424-1804-9 *Building Grammar & Writing Skills*

Name _____ Date _____

Titles Galore

Underline titles of long works such as books, magazines, newspapers, plays,
movies, television shows, CDs, and works of art.

Examples: <u>The Noonday Friends</u> (book)
<u>Cricket</u> (magazine)
<u>Boston Globe</u> (newspaper)

Underline the title in each sentence.

1. Pop and R&B singer, Brandy, is back with a new CD called Full Moon.
2. How to Eat Fried Worms is a book about two boys who try to prove that
   worms make a delicious meal.
3. When my parents go to New York, they are going to see The Phantom of the
   Opera on Broadway.
4. Courage the Cowardly Dog is a TV show about a timid dog who
   acts courageously.
5. The movie, Stuart Little 2, is now playing at the Pacific Theatres in El Segundo.
6. Full Sunlight and Rouen Cathedral are two paintings by Claude Monet that
   show the effect of sunlight on a subject.
7. Write a sentence using the title of your favorite book.

_____

8. Write a sentence using the title of your favorite movie.

_____

9. Write a sentence using the title of your favorite TV show.

_____

10. Write a sentence using the title of your favorite CD.

_____

0-7424-1804-9 *Building Grammar & Writing Skills*

Name _____ Date _____

Pick the Possessive

Add an **apostrophe (') s** to the end of a singular noun to form the possessive.
Example: The boy's bear
Add an **apostrophe (')** to the end of a plural noun to form the possessive.
Example: The kids' backpacks
Add an **apostrophe (') s** to the end of a plural noun that does not end with an *s* to form the possessive.
    The children**'s** lunches

Circle the correct possessive below.

1. My two brother's bikes
   My two brothers' bikes
   My two brothers's bikes

2. The people's umbrellas
   The peoples' umbrellas
   The peoples's umbrellas

3. Each puppy's toys
   Each puppies' toys
   Each puppies's toys

4. Each bosses's desk
   Each bosses' desk
   Each boss's desk

5. My oldest grandfather's cars
   My oldest grandfathers' cars
   My oldest grandfathers's cars

6. The womens' purses
   The women's purses
   The womens's purses

7. An artists' brushes
   An artist's brushes
   An artists's brushes

8. My three sister's room
   My three sisters' room
   My three sisters's room

9. That puppy's dish
   That puppys' dish
   That puppies' dish

10. The mens's jackets
    The mens' jackets
    The men's jackets

11. Rabbit's house
    Rabbits' house
    Rabbits's house

12. Matt's guitar
    Matts' guitar
    Matts's guitar

28

Name _____   Date _____

Marco Polo

Help Cesar proofread his report on Marco Polo. Use the following proofreading marks.

m̲ ≡	Capitalize (6 errors)
/	Lowercase (3 errors)
⊙	Insert period (3 errors)
∧	Insert comma (8 errors)
∨	Insert apostrophe (2 errors)
—	Underline (1 error)

Marco Polo was born in venice in 1254. He was an italian merchant and explorer. He was the first european to cross the entire continent of Asia and leave a record of what he saw and heard.

Marco Polo s father Nicolo Polo was a merchant Nicolo and his brother left on a trading mission to China when Marco was only six years old. Marco was 15 years old by the time his father and uncle returned to Venice. His Mother had died while his father was away and his Aunt and uncle raised him. When he was 17, he accompanied his Father and uncle on a journey to china, traveling along the Silk road and reaching the court of Kublai Khan He served as a government official to Kublai Khan. Their travels took them all over Asia.

The Polos returned to Venice in 1295. They had been gone for 24 years. They brought back many riches—ivory jade jewels, porcelain, silk, and other treasures. However, when they returned, Venice was at war with Genoa In 1296, Marco Polo, a captain of the Venetian galley was captured. While jailed, he dictated to a fellow prisoner what he saw and heard while he traveled. Marco Polo s book The Travels of Marco Polo was one of the most popular books in medieval Europe. Marco Polo died in 1324 when he was 70 years old.

Published by Instructional Fair. Copyright protected.   0-7424-1804-9 *Building Grammar & Writing Skills*

Name _____ Date _____

Parts of Speech Puzzle

Words in sentences can be used in eight different ways. Therefore, there are eight **parts of speech.**

Use the eight parts of speech in the Word Box and the clues below to complete the puzzle.

Word Box			
noun	verb	adjective	adverb
pronoun	preposition	conjunction	interjection

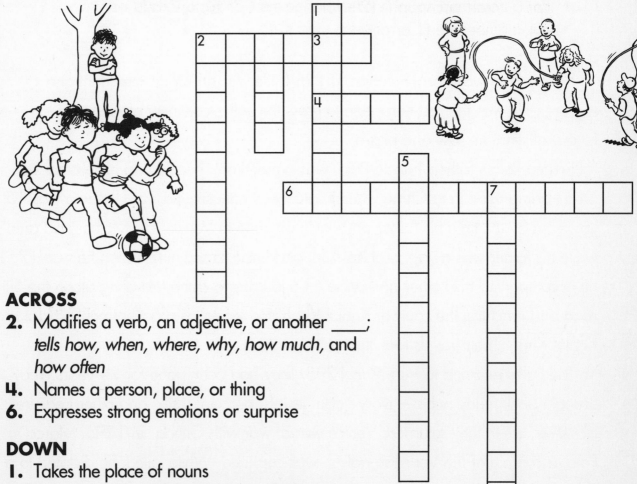

ACROSS

2. Modifies a verb, an adjective, or another ____; *tells how, when, where, why, how much,* and *how often*

4. Names a person, place, or thing

6. Expresses strong emotions or surprise

DOWN

1. Takes the place of nouns

2. Describes or modifies a noun or pronoun

3. Expresses action or indicates a state of being

5. Shows the relationship between a noun or pronoun and another word in the sentence

7. Joins together words, phrases, or clauses

　　　0-7424-1804-9 *Building Grammar & Writing Skills*

Name _____ Date _____

Recipe for Plurals

A **singular noun** names one person, place, thing, or idea.
A **plural noun** names more than one person, place, thing, or idea.
To make plurals, follow these rules:
- Add **s** to most no
- Add **es** to noun ending   z, ch or sh.
- For a noun end ng
- For a noun e ding to   he **y** to **i**, add **es**.
- For a noun   ng   o   f or fe to   , add **es**.
- For a nou   ending
- For a nou
- Some n

Read each n   owing the appropriate rule.

			ey	library
city			x	deer
calf			oth	copy
match	house		mouse	shelf
brush	friend		foot	grocery

Add s	Add es	Change *y* to *i*, add es
_____	_____	_____
_____	_____	_____
_____	_____	_____
_____	_____	_____
_____	_____	

Change *f* or *fe* to *v*, add es	Irregular plurals
_____	_____
_____	_____
_____	_____
_____	_____

0-7424-1804-9 *Building Grammar & Writing Skills*

Name _____ Date _____

Possessives Sort

To make nouns show possession or ownership, follow these rules:
- For singular nouns, add an **apostrophe** and **s**. (*boy–boy's*)
- For plural nouns, add an **apostrophe** after the final **s**. (*girls–girls'*)
- For irregular plural nouns, add an **apostrophe** and **s**. (*children–children's*)

Read each possessive noun. Circle *one* or *more* than one to tell if the possessive is singular or plural.

1. The babies' books   one   more than one
2. The cat's toys   one   more than one
3. The women's gloves   one   more than one
4. The mouse's cheese   one   more than one
5. Jenny's dress   one   more than one
6. The dog's bones   one   more than one
7. The man's guitar   one   more than one
8. The parents' tickets   one   more than one
9. The principals' desks   one   more than one
10. The calves' blankets   one   more than one
11. The child's paintings   one   more than one
12. The queens' jewelry   one   more than one
13. The king's crowns   one   more than one
14. The dinosaurs' boots   one   more than one
15. The bunnies' carrots   one   more than one

0-7424-1804-9 *Building Grammar & Writing Skills*

Name _____ Date _____

Birthday Party

Pronouns take the place of nouns.

I, my, mine, me
we, our, ours, us
he, his, him
she, her, hers
it, its
they, their, theirs, them

Write the correct pronoun for each **boldfaced** word or phrase below.

Last week my sister had a birthday party.

My sister turned 16 years old. She invited 20 friends   1. _____

to go bowling. **She and her friends** had lots of fun.   2. _____

My mom bought prizes for the best bowler,

worst bowler, and best team. Tom was the best. **Tom**   3. _____

scored a 176. Jen was the worst. **Jen** only scored 30!   4. _____

Both Tom and Jen got bowling shirts. **Tom and Jen**   5. _____

really liked **the shirts.** I was on the best bowling team.   6. _____

I and my team scored 788 points. We won **movie**   7. _____

tickets. Everyone said the **movie ticket** was a great gift. 8. _____

After bowling, **everyone at the party** sang   9. _____

"Happy Birthday" to **my sister**. We had ice cream   10. _____

cake and before **everyone** went home. Later, my dad asked 11. _____

us about the party. My sister told **my Dad** it was   12. _____

the best birthday party **my sister** ever had!   13. _____

0-7424-1804-9 *Building Grammar & Writing Skills*

Name _____ Date _____

Pronoun Power

A **subject pronoun** takes the place of a noun in the subject of a sentence.

Example: Charlotte likes math. **She** likes math.

An **object pronoun** takes the place of a noun that receives the action of a verb or follows a preposition such as *to, of,* and *with*.

Examples: Dad told **Kim** about kangaroos. Dad told me about kangaroos.
Vicki took a picture of **the kangaroo.** Vicki took a picture of it.

Subject Pronoun	Object Pronoun
I	me
you	you
he	him
she	her
it	it
we	us
they	them

Read the sentences. Circle the subject pronouns, and underline the object pronouns.

1. On Friday, Darbie and he are going to Seattle to visit Aunt Mable.

2. She is turning 100 years old on Sunday.

3. They have not seen her in over five years.

4. We are picking them up at the airport and taking them to see her.

Write a subject or an object pronoun in place of the **boldfaced** noun(s). Then write *O* or *S* after each sentence to tell if it is a subject pronoun or an object pronoun.

5. _____ Thank you for taking **Kimberly, Noel, and I** to the movies.

6. _____ *Spy Kids 2* was a great movie!

7. _____ I told **Nick** that it would be a good movie.

8. _____ But **Nick** didn't believe me.

34

Name _____ Date _____

It's a Cover-up

A **possessive pronoun** takes the place of a noun that shows possession. **Example: Mrs. Ellison's** hat. **Her** hat.

1. Play this game with a partner. First, each player uses his or her game board (see illustration).

2. Cut out 12 one-inch squares of paper to make playing cards.

3. Write a possessive pronoun on each card: *my, mine, your, yours, his, her, hers, our, ours, their, theirs, its.*

4. To play, place all the cards in a bag.

5. Take turns drawing a card. Find a noun on the game board that can be replaced by the possessive pronoun. Place the card on that square. If an appropriate pronoun is not available, return the card to the bag.

6. The first player to cover four spaces in a row is the winner!

William's room is messy.	**Allison's** car is fast.	That balloon is **Heather's**.	**Callie's and my** bedroom is clean.
The ball is **Philip's** and mine.	**The Sessler's** house is big.	This boat is **the Harrison's**.	**The elephant's** trunk is long.
Mrs. Smith's hair is brown.	These glasses are **Miss Henry's**.	**Mr. Krug's** bike needs repairs.	That is **Tad's** football.

0-7424-1804-9 *Building Grammar & Writing Skills*

Name _____ Date _____

In the Past

Present-tense action verbs tell about actions happening now.
Past-tense action verbs tell about actions that happened in the past.
To change a present-tense verb to a past-tense verb:

- For most verbs, add **ed.** *(snow–snowed)*
- If the verb ends in a silent *e*, drop the **e**, add **ed**. *(like–liked)*
- If the verb ends with a single consonant preceded by a single vowel, double the consonant, add **ed.** *(hug–hugged)*
- If the verb ends in consonant-y, change the **y** to **i**, add **ed.** *(study–studied)*
- Some verbs are irregular. *(think–thought, drink–drank)*

Write the past-tense form of each action verb in the puzzle.

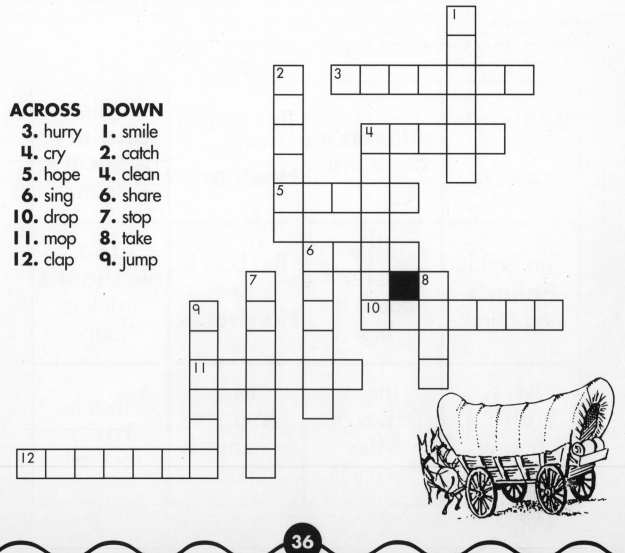

ACROSS	DOWN
3. hurry	**1.** smile
4. cry	**2.** catch
5. hope	**4.** clean
6. sing	**6.** share
10. drop	**7.** stop
11. mop	**8.** take
12. clap	**9.** jump

0-7424-1804-9 *Building Grammar & Writing Skills*

Name _____ Date _____

Go Fish! Verbs Game

Most verbs are made past tense by adding **ed.** But many verbs, such as *eat* are **irregular.**

Examples: Today I'll **eat** pizza for lunch.
Yesterday I **ate** pizza for lunch.
I have already **eaten** pizza for lunch.

Play this game with a partner:

1. Fill in the missing verbs in the chart. Write each verb on a separate index card.

2. Deal seven cards to each player. Place the remaining cards facedown.

3. The object of the game is to make complete sets of irregular verbs.

4. Each player, in turn, asks for a card to complete his or her sets. If the card is not available, the player has to draw from the pile.

5. When all 24 sets are complete, the player with the most complete sets wins!

Present Tense	Past Tense	Past Participle
begin	began	begun
bite	bit	bitten
break	broke	
	brought	brought
catch		caught
choose	chose	
	came	come
drink		drunk
drive	drove	
	flew	flown
give		given
go	went	
	grew	grown
hide		hidden
know	knew	
	rode	ridden
ring		rung
see	saw	
	sang	sung
speak		spoken
swim	swam	
	took	taken
throw		thrown
write	wrote	

37

Name _____ Date _____

A Little Help

Sometimes an action verb gets help from another verb called a **helping verb.**
A helping verb comes before the main verb. It helps tell about an action in the
present, past, or future.

Examples:
Present Tense—am, is, are, have, has, do, does, can
Past Tense—was, were, has, had, did, could
Future—shall, will

Underline the helping verb and circle the main verb in each sentence.

1. Every year the fourth-grade class has visited the nursing home for their
community service project.

2. This year my class is planning something different.

3. We will raise money for the homeless shelter.

4. We have planned several fund-raising activities throughout the school year.

5. In October, Joaquin will give a piano recital.

6. He has played the piano since he was three years old.

7. We are selling tickets for two dollars each.

8. We are also collecting bottles and cans.

9. Mr. and Mrs. Chang have donated recycling containers to place around school.

10. I am writing an announcement for the principal to read during the morning
message.

11. Ronald and Nan are making flyers.

12. Hector shall post them around the neighborhood.

0-7424-1804-9 *Building Grammar & Writing Skills*

Name _____ Date _____

A Tall Tale

Most verbs name actions. The verb **be** is different. It tells about someone or something. It can also act as a helping verb.

Read the sentences. Fill in the blanks with a form of the verb **be**: *am, is, are, was, were, be, being,* or *been.*

1. My brother Earl _____ as tall as the Washington Monument.

2. When he was born, his lungs _____ so strong that he could blow up a hot-air balloon in one puff.

3. Earl's clothing _____ so large they had to use hubcaps for buttons.

4. His shoes _____ made from the trunks of redwoods.

5. When he _____ sleeping, he snored so loudly that the shingles would come off the roof.

6. Earl's pet elephant, Esther, _____ purple with pink polka dots.

7. Esther's footsteps _____ so heavy, they shook the earth.

8. That's how the Rocky Mountains _____ formed.

9. When Earl was five, Esther and he had _____ caught in a tornado.

10. But Esther was good at _____ resourceful.

11. She wrapped that tornado into a knot with her trunk, and it _____ flung into space.

12. That's how the first rocket came to _____!

0-7424-1804-9 *Building Grammar & Writing Skills*

Name _____ Date _____

Lots of Links

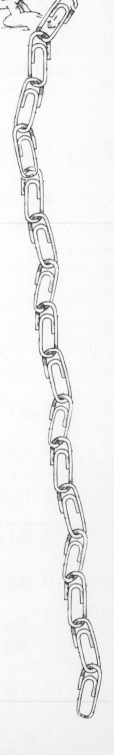

Linking verbs link the subject of a sentence to a noun or adjective in the predicate. They help tell us what the subject is. Common linking verbs include: *am, is, are, was, were, smell, look, taste, remain, feel, appear,* and *become.*

Underline the linking verb in each sentence. Then draw an arrow to "link" the subject to the noun or adjective in the predicate.

1. New York is a city.

2. Jason appeared happy when he won the race.

3. The fourth graders are very excited for the field trip.

4. The spaghetti tastes delicious.

5. Everybody stayed calm when the fire alarm went off.

6. Victor sounded very surprised when he won the writing contest.

7. The best swimmers were Margie and Cathie.

8. Elizabeth seems happy to be back home.

9. Grandma looks really tired.

10. Mehrad's brother became a doctor.

11. The monkey looked hungry.

12. I am excited because tomorrow is my birthday!

40

Name _____ Date _____

Describing Details

An **adjective** is a word that describes a noun or pronoun.
An adjective tells **how many, what kind, and which ones**.

Examples: Two monsters
             Loveable monsters
             Polka-dotted monsters
Write three descriptive adjectives for each noun.

1. Bear
_____
_____
_____

2. Summer
_____
_____
_____

3. Clown
_____
_____
_____

4. Flower
_____
_____
_____

5. School
_____
_____
_____

6. Baby
_____
_____
_____

7. Pizza
_____
_____
_____

8. Car
_____
_____
_____

Choose four nouns above. Then write a sentence using each noun and
your adjectives.

9. _____

10. _____

11. _____

12. _____

41

Name _____ Date _____

Let's Compare

Adjectives that compare two things usually end in **er**.
Adjectives that compare three or more things usually end in **est**.

Examples: The cat is **small**.
The mouse is **smaller** than the cat.
The spider is the **smallest** of all.

Write sentences using these comparative adjectives and nouns.

1. fastest car

_____

2. smaller cookie

_____

3. quicker horse

_____

4. slowest truck

_____

5. higher building

_____

6. ugliest monster

_____

7. taller girl

_____

8. brighter lamp

_____

9. cleanest shirt

_____

10. friendliest dog

_____

0-7424-1804-9 *Building Grammar & Writing Skills*

Name _____ Date _____

Assorted Adverbs

An **adverb** is a word that tells more about a verb. An adverb may tell **how** something is done (*quickly, slowly*), **when** it is done (*yesterday, later*), or **where** it is done (*away, inside*).

Circle the adverb in each sentence. Then cut apart the sentences. On a separate sheet of paper, write the titles: *How? When?* and *Where?* Arrange the sentence strips under the appropriate titles to show if the adverb tells how, when, or where.

She sings beautifully.	We will meet here after the movie.
The party will take place here.	Stacey can clearly see the road signs.
Hector talked quietly to his sister.	The water flowed rapidly.
Now it's time to open the presents!	I left my gloves somewhere.
The cat crept slowly to the fence.	Pam will know the answer soon.
Today we will visit our grandparents.	Let's go home.
Put the box there, on the table.	Jeremy hopped over the puddle.
Erin's story will be published later.	Cassie scratched Rover's ear softly.
Emily often orders plain spaghetti.	Katie is always late to dance class.
I carefully washed the expensive vase.	We cheered happily when she won.
I'll check out of the hotel tomorrow.	I want to go over to that museum.
The lake was nearby.	Jenna laughed loudly at the funny clown.
It was too soon to tell.	The clever fox hid behind the tree.

43

Name _____ Date _____

Merely Modifying

Adjectives and **adverbs** make the meaning of other words clearer and more specific. Adjectives modify nouns and pronouns. Adverbs modify verbs.

Examples: Mary is a **slow** runner. (adjective)
Mary runs **slowly**. (adverb)

Write whether each boldfaced word is an adjective or adverb. Then write another sentence using the same adjective or adverb.

1. My grandparents have a **small** house. _____

_____

2. Anita plays the piano **beautifully**. _____

_____

3. Mr. Henderson dresses **casually**. _____

_____

4. The soup is very **hot**. _____

_____

5. The microwave can cook food **fast**. _____

_____

6. She is an **intelligent** woman. _____

_____

7. James walks **quickly** to school. _____

_____

8. I am going to the circus **tomorrow**. _____

_____

44

Name _____ Date _____

Preposition Puzzle

Pepositions link and relate a noun or pronoun to another word in a sentence. Common prepositions include: *in, on, up, for, at, by, of, with, to, before,* and *after.*

Underline the preposition in each sentence, and then circle it in the puzzle.

1. He scattered his clothes around the bedroom.
2. The rabbit is underneath the rock.
3. Rodney walked into the wrong classroom.
4. Can you eat soup without a spoon?
5. Hector lives across the street.
6. This present is for Greg.
7. Heather is hiding under the chair.
8. Casey stored her winter clothes inside a large box.
9. We will stay at the beach until it is dark.
10. Christopher walked through the forest.
11. The horse jumped over the bushes.
12. The thank-you note is from my niece.
13. Stan laughed during the whole movie.
14. Mom planted a garden behind our house

```
D I J T R L B S M D D O C I O L W G L H
U G N E U E I G B N I T X P A O D O P G
R V V S H O D T U R I N R E D N U V W U
I O M I I A H O N J A I F P E W W E M O
N Y N S R D R T Y U W O V O T X E R W R
G D I U K A E P I H T A E N R E D N U H
H S K L G L X K M W V S A C R O S S C T
Z T Z F R O M R N R Q M Z X N K V R M C
```

45

Name _____ Date _____

Conjunction Function

A **conjunction** joins together words, phrases, or clauses. Common conjunctions include: *and, but, or, for, yet,* and *so.*

I have dogs **and** cats as pets. (words)
Let's go to the movies **or** the mall. (phrases)
I will get wet, **for** it is raining. (clauses)

_____ **and** _____

Circle the conjunction in each sentence.
On the line, identify what the conjunction is joining—*words, phrases,* or *clauses.*

1. _____ The train is long and slow.

2. _____ Nancy lost her watch at the beach or the park.

3. _____ We left on Thursday, but we didn't come back until Tuesday.

4. _____ I want to sit in the front row, so I ordered my tickets early.

5. _____ Hiran won the 5K race, for he is an excellent runner.

6. _____ The day was cloudy, yet warm.

7. _____ Today, Sonja is playing tennis and going swimming.

8. _____ Logan may watch television or read a book.

9. _____ Mom wants to go out to eat, yet Dad wants to eat at home.

10. _____ Jesse can do a cartwheel but not a round-off.

11. _____ Aunt Kerry will bake or buy the cake.

12. _____ Rachel is hungry, so she made a sandwich to eat.

13. _____ My kindergartners learned how to hop and skip.

14. _____ Mom put salt on the sidewalk, so the ice will melt.

0-7424-1804-9 *Building Grammar & Writing Skills*

Name _____ Date _____

Awesome Interjections!

Interjections are words that express strong feelings. An interjection is usually followed by an exclamation point.

Circle the interjection in each sentence.

1. Hey! Look at the size of that roller coaster.

2. Wow! It has to be over 200 feet high!

3. Oh yeah! Let's get in line for a ride.

4. No way! I am not riding that coaster.

5. Hurry! The line is getting longer.

6. Oh dear! I think I might be ill.

7. Yikes! This is taller than I thought.

8. Eeeeeek! I am scared.

9. Ah! Here comes another big hill, and we're facing backwards.

10. Whoa! Hold on tight.

11. Whew! We made it.

12. Awesome! That was the best roller coaster ride!

Write a sentence with an interjection, using each emotion below.

13. mad _____

14. happy _____

15. excited _____

0-7424-1804-9 *Building Grammar & Writing Skills*

Name _____ Date _____

The Plural Express

A **plural noun** names more than one person, place, thing, or idea.
- Add **s** to most nouns.
- Add **es** to nouns ending in *s, x, z, ch* or *sh*.
- For a noun ending in vowel-*y*, add **s**.
- For a noun ending in consonant-*y*, change the **y** to **i**, add **es**.
- For a noun ending in *f* or *fe*, change the **f** or **fe** to **v**, add **es**.
- For a noun ending in vowel-*o*, add **s**.
- For a noun ending in consonant-*o*, add **es**.
- Some nouns have irregular plurals. *(child–children)*

Write the correct plural nouns to complete each sentence.

1. There were six (turkey) _____ and two (goose) _____ in the petting zoo.

2. We bought a bouquet of (daisy) _____ and some (peach) _____ at the farmer's market.

3. Three (shelf) _____ in the china cabinet held water (glass) _____ .

4. Four (man) _____ chased seven (deer) _____ through the forest.

5. That mountain range has numerous (peak) _____ and (valley) _____ .

6. Jenny was one of five (child) _____ in her family to go to these (university) _____ .

7. Brad wanted three (mouse) _____ and two (fish) _____ for his birthday.

8. We traveled to two big (city) _____ and saw three famous (museum) _____ .

9. Those (cow) _____ gave birth to seven (calf) _____ all together.

10. Jessica's (sister) _____ threw two big graduation (party) _____ .

11. I packed 10 (box) _____ of flowers, 50 (bunch) _____ in all!

12. Tyrese hid in the (bush) _____ after he broke Mom's (dish) _____ .

48

0-7424-1804-9 *Building Grammar & Writing Skills*

Name _____ Date _____

It's Mine!

A noun is **possessive** when it shows possession or ownership.
- For a possessive singular noun, add **apostrophe** and **s**. *(cat's)*
- For a possessive plural noun, add an **apostrophe**. *(cats')*
- For a possessive, irregular plural noun, add an **apostrophe** and **s**. *(women's)*

Fill in the circle beside the correct plural noun to complete each sentence.

1. Two _____ were fighting over my shoe. ○ puppies ○ puppy's ○ puppies'

2. A _____ toy truck was missing. ○ boys ○ boy's ○ boys'

3. Three _____ computers were new. ○ students ○ student's ○ students'

4. The _____ were blue. ○ shoes ○ shoe's ○ shoes'

5. _____ hats are now on sale. ○ Ladies ○ Ladies's ○ Ladies'

6. Two _____ have red noses. ○ clowns ○ clown's ○ clowns'

7. The _____ restroom is on the first floor. ○ women ○ women's ○ womens'

8. Four _____ galloped in the field. ○ horses ○ horse's ○ horses'

9. Five _____ jackets were green. ○ girls ○ girl's ○ girls'

10. That _____ tail is curly. ○ dogs ○ dog's ○ dogs'

11. Alex forgot to water _____ plants. ○ Moms ○ Mom's ○ Moms'

12. Did you see those _____ jump? ○ dolphins ○ dolphins' ○ dolphin's

13. The _____ parties are on Monday. ○ classes ○ classes's ○ classes'

14. That _____ shell is very large. ○ turtles ○ turtle's ○ turtles'

49

Name _____ Date _____

At the Movies

Iggy and Wiggy have trouble using pronouns. Help them correct each sentence. Write **C** if the pronoun is used correctly. Write **X** if the pronoun is not used correctly. Then rewrite the sentence using the correct pronoun.

Subject Pronoun	Object Pronoun
I	me
she	her
he	him

1. ___ Me and Iggy are going to the movies. _____

2. ___ Her and I bought popcorn. _____

3. ___ Me like butter on popcorn. _____

4. ___ Iggy will sit between Wiggy and he. _____

5. ___ Iggy told he the movie was funny. _____

6. ___ He did not think the movie was funny. _____

7. ___ Please give me some popcorn. _____

8. ___ Him saw the movie five times. _____

9. ___ She asked Wiggy to move over. _____

10. ___ Wiggy wants she to him buy a drink. _____

11. ___ Iggy will not buy him a drink. _____

12. ___ Wiggy and me didn't like the movie. _____

13. ___ Wiggy often goes to the movies with I. _____

14. ___ She and I will go to the movies next Saturday. _____

0-7424-1804-9 *Building Grammar & Writing Skills*

Name _____ Date _____

Confusing Words

Iggy and Wiggy need help using pronouns and contractions. Fill in the circle beside the word that correctly finishes each sentence.

Possessive Pronoun	Contraction
your (belongs to you)	you're (you are)
their (belongs to them)	they're (they are)
its (belongs to it)	it's (it is)

1. Iggy said, "_____ my best friend."

  ○ Your   ○ You're

2. _____ my turn to take you out to eat.

  ○ Its   ○ It's

3. _____ engine blew up.

  ○ Its   ○ It's

4. They are taking _____ spacecraft to the repair shop.

  ○ their   ○ they're

5. The repairman told Iggy _____ beyond repair.

  ○ its   ○ it's

6. I think _____ going to have to buy a new spacecraft.

  ○ your   ○ you're

7. _____ going shopping tomorrow.

  ○ Their   ○ They're

8. Did you know _____ mom is waiting for you?

  ○ your   ○ you're

9. Mom said, "Don't forget to bring _____ money."

  ○ your   ○ you're

10. Iggy and Wiggy will use the money for _____ new spacecraft.

  ○ their   ○ they're

0-7424-1804-9 *Building Grammar & Writing Skills*

Name _____ Date _____

Let's Agree

Present-tense verbs that tell about one person or thing have an **s** or **es** at the end.
Examples: Wesley **jumps** over the hurdle.
Julie **washes** the car.

Present-tense verbs that tell about more than one person or thing, or follow the pronouns *you or I*, do not have an **s** or **es** at the end.
Examples: Rita and Wesley **jump** over the hurdle.
I wash the car.

Fill in the circle beside the correct present-tense verb.

1. I ____ the guitar and drums.	O play	O plays
2. Sammy ____ at the neighbor's cat.	O bark	O barks
3. My little brothers ____ a great deal of noise.	O make	O makes
4. My sisters ____ their Irish dancing.	O practice	O practices
5. Will you ____ the cake for Randi's birthday?	O bake	O bakes
6. Colleen and Victor ____ before running.	O stretch	O stretches
7. Pat's dog ____ every car and truck.	O chase	O chases
8. Oliver ____ along the pathway.	O skate	O skates
9. Deanna and Lannie ____ to school.	O walk	O walks
10. Kim and Pam always ____ at my jokes.	O laugh	O laughs
11. Can you ____ ?	O skip	O skips
12. Steven ____ the high fly ball to left field.	O catch	O catches

0-7424-1804-9 *Building Grammar & Writing Skills*

Name _____ Date _____

Write It Right

Read each sentence. Then rewrite the sentence correctly, using the proper past-tense irregular verb. Read aloud the corrected sentence.

1. **Wrong:** I goed to my grandmother's house.
   Correct: <u>I went to my grandmother's house.</u>

2. **Wrong:** My sister breaked my mom's watch.
   Correct: _____

3. **Wrong:** I catched the ball.
   Correct: _____

4. **Wrong**: My class readed 145 books for the reading contest.
   Correct: _____

5. **Wrong:** I was so thirsty that I drinked the whole glass of water!
   Correct: _____

6. **Wrong:** We swimmed in my aunt's pool all day.
   Correct: _____

7. **Wrong:** Mom, Leslie taked my dinosaur.
   Correct: _____

8. **Wrong:** My grandpa teached me how to ride a bike.
   Correct: _____

9. **Wrong:** Dad, Bill throwed the baseball right through that window!
   Correct: _____

10. **Wrong:** Emily bringed her baseball cards to school for show-and-tell.
    Correct: _____

11. **Wrong:** My little sister drawed all over my science project.
    Correct: _____

12. **Wrong:** She teared my math homework in half, too.
    Correct: _____

0-7424-1804-9 *Building Grammar & Writing Skills*

Name _____ Date _____

Talent Show

Some verbs are **irregular**. They form their past tenses and
participles in irregular ways.
    Present: I **bite** the apple.
    Past: Yesterday, I **bit** the apple.
    Past Participle: Last year, I had **bitten** the apple.

Fill in the circle beside the sentence that uses the boldfaced verb correctly. If the verb
is used incorrectly, write the proper verb on the line.
Hint: A past participle is used with the helping verbs *have, has,* or *had.*

o **1.** Last Friday night, Lincoln Elementary School **had** a talent show. _____

o **2.** Many parents and relatives had **came** to see the children perform. _____

o **3.** The show **began** with the fifth-grade band. _____

o **4.** They **given** a five-minute concert. _____

o **5.** Stephanie, a second grader, **sing** a song. _____

o **6.** Hector recited a poem he had **wrote**. _____

o **7.** Jack **rode** a unicycle in circles while juggling five balls. _____

o **8.** Alice had **thrown** all four knives in the bulls-eye from 30 feet. _____

o **9.** Her relatives **known** that she would be great. _____

o **10.** They had **driven** across country to watch her perform. _____

o **11.** I **done** several magic tricks. _____

o **12.** Before I had **went** on stage, I saw my parents sitting in the front row. _____

o **13.** I got so nervous that I **bit** my tongue. _____

o **14.** I almost **forgotten** to put my rabbit in my hat. _____

o **15.** I **gotten** third place in the Talent Show! _____

54

0-7424-1804-9 *Building Grammar & Writing Skills*

Name _____ Date _____

A Monster Challenge

Oogly and Doodly have trouble using the verbs *lay* and *lie* correctly. So, Doodly is challenging Oogly to a verb game!

Lay means to *put or place something or someone down.*
   Example: Carlyle **lays** the cordless phone on the table.
Lie means to *rest or recline.*
   Example: Isaac **lies** in the middle of the exercise mat.

Help Oogly and Doodly use *lay* and *lie* correctly.
Fill in the circle next to the correct verb.

1. You will feel better if you ___ down.
   ○ lay
   ○ lie

2. _____ the books on the table.
   ○ Lay
   ○ Lie

3. The chickens will not _____ any eggs.
   ○ lay
   ○ lie

4. I told my dog to _____ down on the porch.
   ○ lay
   ○ lie

5. My hamster _____ in his nest all day.
   ○ lays
   ○ lies

6. My teacher _____ her papers on the desk.
   ○ lays
   ○ lies

7. The cat _____ in the flowerbed.
   ○ lays
   ○ lies

8. Kirsten _____ her head on her desk.
   ○ lays
   ○ lies

9. Henry _____ on the couch to watch TV.
   ○ lays
   ○ lies

10. _____ the guests' coats on the bed.
   ○ Lay
   ○ Lie

11. My cat loves to _____ on my pillow.
   ○ lay
   ○ lie

12. Mom _____ my baby sister in the crib.
   ○ lays
   ○ lies

55

Name _____ Date _____

Read-a-Thon

A **helping verb** comes before the main verb. It helps tell about an action in the present, past, or future.

Read these sentences. Then write the correct helping verb in parentheses.

1. Nottingham Elementary School _____ holding its annual reading contest. (is/are)

2. They _____ held this contest for seven years. (has/have)

3. The contest _____ held for one month. (is/are)

4. Each class _____ setting a goal for the number of books read. (is/are)

5. This student _____ keeping a list of the books she reads. (is/are)

6. At the end of the first week, Mrs. Cantu's class _____ read a total of 50 books. (had/have).

7. Steven and Mary _____ trying to read the most books. (was/were)

8. However, they _____ only read two books each, while Anthony _____ read four. (has/had)

9. By the end of the second week, Steven _____ read the most books in his class. (do/did)

10. But, by the end of the third week, Mary _____ read the most books. (had/have)

11. Mrs. Cantu's class _____ read 320 books in a month. (has/have)

12. The class _____ raised over three hundred dollars. (has/have)

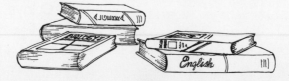

56

0-7424-1804-9 *Building Grammar & Writing Skills*

Name _____ Date _____

Adjective Wise

Adjectives that compare two things usually end in **er**.
Adjectives that compare three or more things usually end in **est**.
But if the adjective has more than two syllables, add *more* or *most*.

Examples: The blue vase is **beautiful**.
The pink vase is **more beautiful** than the blue one.
The green vase is the **most beautiful** of all.

Read each sentence. Then write the correct adjective in parentheses.

1. This math book has the _____ problems of all. (hard)

2. Mindy thinks that SpongeBob SquarePants is the _____ show
   on TV. (funny)

3. California is _____ to the Pacific Ocean than Kansas. (close)

4. A toucan is _____ than a crow. (colorful)

5. Sirius is the _____ star of all! (bright)

6. The judges voted Grandma's blueberry pie the _____
   in the contest. (delicious)

7. Alex thinks that math is _____ than reading. (interesting)

8. A python is _____ than a Braminy blind snake. (long)

9. Dad wrote the _____ directions of all. (confusing)

10. Kayla is _____ at ballet than tap dancing. (graceful)

11. Peaches are _____ than lemons. (sweet)

12. Farmer Fred's _____ moment was coming in last in
    the turkey-calling contest. (embarrassing)

0-7424-1804-9 *Building Grammar & Writing Skills*

Name _____ Date _____

Adverb Adventure

An **adverb** is a word that tells more about a verb.
An adverb may tell **how** something is done *(quietly, happily)*, **when** it is done *(today, later)*, or **where** it is done *(up, inside)*.

Use the clues and the adverbs in the Word Box to complete the puzzle.

Word Box					
away	swiftly	late	suddenly	daily	soon
carefully	noisily	there	everywhere	here	extremely

ACROSS

1. The tiger ____ roared, scaring us.
3. The children talked ____ before the magic show began.
6. The poodles jumped ____ through the Hula-Hoops.
10. Put the books ____ on the table.
11. A kangaroo can leap ____ high.

DOWN

2. He plays the guitar ____ at the coffee shop.
4. We arrived ____ at the fair.
5. Grandma still lives ____.
6. We will go to the circus ____.
7. The dog searched for the bone ___.
8. The acrobat walked ____ across the tightrope.
9. The dove flew____ from the magician.

0-7424-1804-9 *Building Grammar & Writing Skills*

Name _____ Date _____

Troubling Words

Good is an adjective. It is used when describing a noun or pronoun.
   Example: Mindy and Mandy are very **good** friends.
Well is an adverb. It is used when describing a verb.
   Example: Mindy plays **well** with all the other bears.

Mindy and Mandy have trouble using *good* and *well*. Help them fill in the
circle next to the correct adjective or adverb for each sentence.

1. Mindy is a _____ dancer.
   O good   O well

2. Mandy sings very _____.
   O good   O well

3. Mindy can't hear very _____.
   O good   O well

4. Mindy is a _____ singer, too.
   O good   O well

5. Mandy plays the flute _____ in
the band.
   O good   O well

6. Mindy is not a very ____ drummer.
   O good   O well

7. Mandy can play the piano _____.
   O good   O well

8. Mandy and Mindy are____students.
   O good   O well

9. Mindy always studies _____.
   O good   O well

10. Like most bears, Mandy is a
_____ actor.
   O good   O well

11. Mindy doesn't cook _____.
   O good   O well

12. Mandy is a very _____ worker.
   O good   O well

13. Mandy is doing very ___,
thank you.
   O good   O well

14. Mindy plays soccer _____.
   O good   O well

   0-7424-1804-9 *Building Grammar & Writing Skills*

Name _____ Date _____

Peppy Prepositions

Prepositions link and relate a noun or pronoun to another word in a sentence.
Examples: The cow jumped **over** the moon.
Bernie was **on** the volleyball team.

Use the prepositions in the Word Box to complete the puzzle.

Word Box					
among	past	toward	into	after	against
near	before	down	about	since	until

ACROSS

2. Becky cannot watch TV ____ she does her homework.
4. Clifford drove ____ the highway.
7. ____ school, Paula has ballet lessons.
8. Ethan will not go swimming ____ it is raining.
11. Irene is standing ____ the roses.
12. Seth rolled ____ the hill.

DOWN

1. The movie was ____ a lost puppy.
3. The bull charged ____ the cowboy.
5. Tam hit the tennis ball ____ the garage door.
6. Louis must wash the dishes ____ watching TV.
9. ____ the bridge, there is a large oak tree.
10. Jeff and Julie dove ____ the swimming pool.

0-7424-1804-9 *Building Grammar & Writing Skills*

Name _____ Date _____

Where's the Animal?

Prepositions are usually found in phrases. A **prepositional phrase** is a group of words that begins with a preposition and ends with a noun.

    Examples: The cat is **outside the box**.
                  The horse is **between the stalls**.

Complete each sentence by writing a prepositional phrase that describes the picture.

1. The goat _____.

2. A fox _____.

3. An elephant _____.

4. The giraffes _____.

5. The cat _____.

6. The rabbit _____.

    0-7424-1804-9 *Building Grammar & Writing Skills*

Name _____ Date _____

Let's Connect

Conjunctions, such as *and* and *or*, can connect two or more simple subjects to form a compound subject.

    Example: Sallie loves to talk. Roberto loves to talk. (and)
               Sallie **and** Roberto love to talk.

Use a **conjunction** (*and, or*) to write a sentence with a compound subject.

1. Renee likes pudding for dessert. Michel likes pudding for dessert.

_____

2. Kim is leaving on Friday. Nicholas is leaving on Friday.

_____

3. Jose will answer the question. Rebecca will answer the question.

_____

4. Randy will make cookies. Sean will make cookies. Rudy will make cookies.

_____

Conjunctions, such as *and*, *but*, and *or*, can connect two or more simple predicates to form a compound predicate.

    Example: The dog jumps high. The dog runs slowly. (but)
               The dog jumps high **but** runs slowly.

Use a conjunction (*and, but, or*) to write a sentence with a compound predicate.

5. The day was sunny. The day was warm.

_____

6. Tina will play hopscotch. Tina will play tag.

_____

7. Freddie washed his car. Freddie waxed his car.

_____

    0-7424-1804-9 *Building Grammar & Writing Skills*

Name _____ Date _____

Writing Strategies

Choose a **topic** for your writing.
- *What am I writing about?*

Decide on a **purpose** for writing.
- *Why am I writing this piece?*
- *What do I hope the audience will learn from reading this piece?*

Identify your **audience**.
- *Who am I writing to?*

Decide on a writing **style**.
- *Expository*—Gives information or explains facts or ideas
- *Persuasive*—Tries to talk someone into something
- *Narrative*—Tells a story
- *Descriptive*—Presents a clear picture of a person, place, thing, or idea

Decide on a **genre**—essay, letter, poetry, autobiography, fiction, nonfiction

Decide on a **point of view**—first person, second person, or third person

Brainstorm by listing or drawing your main ideas.

Use a graphic organizer to organize your thoughts.

Revise, revise, revise!

- Use **descriptive words.**
- Use **transitions** and linking expressions.
- Use a **variety of sentence structures.**
- **Elaborate** with facts and details.
- Group your ideas into **paragraphs**.
- **Proofread** for capitalization, punctuation, and spelling.

63

Name _____ Date _____

My Topic and Purpose

When choosing a topic for writing, it important to know your **purpose** as well as your **audience**.

Draw a line to match each topic with the appropriate purpose and audience.

Purpose & Audience

- Purpose: to entertain
  Audience: classmates and teachers

- Purpose: to talk someone into something (persuade)
  Audience: voters

- Purpose: to give information
  Audience: skateboarders

- Purpose: to talk someone into something (persuade)
  Audience: mom and dad

- Purpose: to provide information
  Audience: science fair judges

- Purpose: to explain
  Audience: chefs

- Purpose: to give information
  Audience: little brother

Topics

- Why does a dog make a good pet?

- How to get good grades

- Support me for president.

- How a liquid changes into a gas

- What are the advantages and disadvantages to wearing a helmet?

- What if you found a dinosaur in your backyard?

- How to make an apple pie

0-7424-1804-9 *Building Grammar & Writing Skills*

Name _____ Date _____

Writing Styles

Sometimes you are given an idea or starting point for writing. This is called a **prompt**. From the prompt, you must determine what is being asked and what style of writing is required. Some styles of writing include:

Expository writing gives information or explains facts or ideas.
Persuasive writing tries to talk someone into something.
Narrative writing tells a story.
Descriptive writing presents a clear picture of a person, place, thing, or idea.

Read each prompt. Then write the style of writing required—*expository, persuasive, narrative, or descriptive.*

1. _____ Write an essay telling how to ride a bicycle.

2. _____ Write an essay that convinces the reader that students should have physical education classes everyday.

3. _____ Write a report explaining why some places have tornadoes and others do not.

4. _____ Imagine you and your friend were chosen to go on a space shuttle to Mars. How would you feel? What might you see? What problems might you encounter? Write a story about your adventure.

5. _____ Think about your favorite place. Use your five senses to describe it.

6. _____ Write an essay that convinces people to save the rain forests.

7. _____ Think of your favorite food. How does is taste? Smell? Look? Write a description of your favorite food.

8. _____ Think about the time when you first learned to ride a bike. How old were you? Where were you? Who else was there? Write a paragraph about your experience.

 0-7424-1804-9 *Building Grammar & Writing Skills*

Graphic Organizers

A **graphic organizer** is used to organize information in the prewriting stage of the writing process. It is a diagram in which you can list key words or phrases about your main idea and supporting details. Here are two kinds of graphic organizers.

In this graphic organizer, the main idea is written in the center circle. The supporting details are written on the lines around the circle. Use these supporting details to complete this graphic organizer.

Supporting Details
Mammal
Marsupial
Australia and neighboring islands
Carry young in pouch
Baby is called a joey
Hind legs and tail for hopping
Largest kangaroos, gray and red

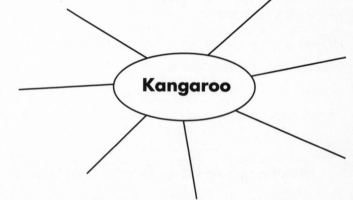

Use the main idea and supporting details to complete this graphic organizer.

Main Idea and Supporting Details
Red kangaroo
Largest species
Varies in color from brick red to gray
Found in desert areas of Australia

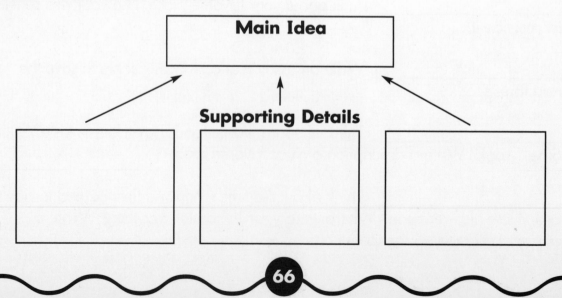

0-7424-1804-9 *Building Grammar & Writing Skills*

Name _____ Date _____

Organize Your Outline

An **outline** is used for organizing information in a logical order in the prewriting stage of the writing process. It includes key words or phrases to show main topics, subtopics, and specific details. An outline can be used for most styles of compositions, including reports, narratives, and summaries.

The **main topics** are the major points in your outline. Main topics are labeled with a Roman numeral *(I, II, III)*, and the first word is capitalized.

Read each group of subtopics. Then write a main topic on the line.

1. I. _____
- **A.** Tulip
- **B.** Daisy
- **C.** Rose
- **D.** Daffodil

II. _____
- **A.** Oak
- **B.** Maple
- **C.** Redwood
- **D.** Pine

3. I. _____
- **A.** Tuna
- **B.** Bass
- **C.** Trout
- **D.** Shark

II. _____
- **A.** Clam
- **B.** Crab
- **C.** Lobster
- **D.** Shrimp

5. I. _____
- **A.** Pig
- **B.** Horse
- **C.** Cow
- **D.** Duck

II. _____
- **A.** Bear
- **B.** Lion
- **C.** Tiger
- **D.** Elephant

2. I. _____
- **A.** Peach
- **B.** Pear
- **C.** Watermelon
- **D.** Apple

II. _____
- **A.** Broccoli
- **B.** Lima Beans
- **C.** Lettuce
- **D.** Asparagus

4. I. _____
- **A.** Robin
- **B.** Quail
- **C.** Cardinal
- **D.** Blue jay

II. _____
- **A.** Bee
- **B.** Butterfly
- **C.** Ant
- **D.** Grasshopper

67

Name _____ Date _____

Many Musical Instruments

The **subtopics** in an **outline** are grouped under and related to the main topics. Subtopics provide more information about the main topic. Subtopics are labeled with capital letters (A, B, C), and the first word is capitalized.

Read the main topics. Then use the words in the Word Box to list the correct subtopics.

Word Box

Trombone	Saxophone	Snare drum	French horn	Piccolo
Kettledrum	Clarinet	Bugle	Cello	Harpsichord
Bass drum	Piano	Violin	Bass	Cymbals
Flute	Harp	Organ	Trumpet	

I. Percussion Instruments
  A. Kettledrum
  B. _____
  C. _____
  D. _____

IV. Woodwind Instruments
  A. _____
  B. _____
  C. _____
  D. _____

II. Brass Instruments
  A. _____
  B. _____
  C. _____
  D. _____

V. Keyboard Instruments
  A. _____
  B. _____
  C. _____
  D. _____

III. Stringed Instruments
  A. _____
  B. _____
  C. _____
  D. _____

0-7424-1804-9 *Building Grammar & Writing Skills*

Name _____ Date _____

What Is It?

The **title** in an **outline** is written at the top of the outline.
Read the paragraph. Then complete the outline by writing the title, main topics, and subtopics.

Have you ever wondered what the difference is between a yam and sweet potato? I always thought they were the same, but they aren't. Yams and sweet potatoes come from different plant families. The yam belongs to the yam family, while the sweet potato belongs to the morning-glory family. When you eat a yam or sweet potato, you are eating different parts of the plant. When you eat a yam, you are eating its tuber; when you eat a sweet potato, you are eating the storage root. Another difference is in their appearance. A yam is long and cylinder-shaped, and has rough and scaly skin. Whereas, a sweet potato is short and block-shaped, with tapered ends. It has smooth, thin skin. Furthermore, a yam tastes starchy, while a sweet potato tastes sweet. Lastly, yams require hot, moist weather and a long growing season. That is why yams aren't grown in the United States. However, sweet potatoes can be grown in cooler climates, like the United States. Now, if anyone asks you what the difference is between a yam and sweet potato, you will have the answer!

Title: _____

   I. _____

       A. _____

       B. _____

       C. _____

       D. _____

       E. _____

0-7424-1804-9 *Building Grammar & Writing Skills*

Name _____ Date _____

Details, Details

The **details** in an **outline** are grouped under the subtopics. Details are labeled with numbers (*1, 2, 3*), and the first word is capitalized.

Read the main topics and subtopics. Then use the words in the Word Box to list the correct details.

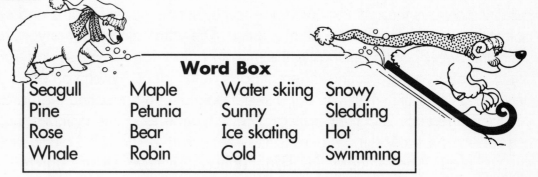

Word Box

Seagull	Maple	Water skiing	Snowy
Pine	Petunia	Sunny	Sledding
Rose	Bear	Ice skating	Hot
Whale	Robin	Cold	Swimming

I. Plants

    A. Trees
        1. _____

        2. _____

    B. Flowers
        1. _____

        2. _____

II. Animals

    A. Mammals
        1. _____

        2. _____

    B. Birds
        1. _____

        2. _____

I. Winter

    A. Weather
        1. _____

        2. _____

    B. Activities
        1. _____

        2. _____

II. Summer

    A. Weather
        1. _____

        2. _____

    B. Activities
        1. _____

        2. _____

0-7424-1804-9 *Building Grammar & Writing Skills*

Name _____ Date _____

Wild Kingdom

An **outline** is used for organizing information in the prewriting stage of the writing process. It includes key words or phrases for main topics, subtopics, and specific details.

Use the words in the Word Box to complete the outline below. Find main topics, subtopics, and details.

Classification of Animals

I. _____

   A. _____

      1. _____

      2. _____

   B. _____

      1. _____

      2. _____

   C. _____

      1. _____

      2. _____

II. _____

   A. _____

      1. _____

      2. _____

      3. _____

   B. _____

   C. _____

Word Box

Spiders
Vertebrates
Jellyfish
Mammals
Ants
Giraffes
Invertebrates
Amphibians
Dragonflies
Alligators
Foxes
Insects
Frogs
Reptiles
Crocodiles
Salamanders
Butterflies

0-7424-1804-9 *Building Grammar & Writing Skills*

Name _____ Date _____

What's the Point?

A **paragraph** is a group of related sentences about one
topic. A paragraph has:

- a main idea
- a topic sentence
- supporting sentences
- a closing sentence

The **main idea** of a paragraph is the most important point the author is trying to
make about the topic. All the sentences in the paragraph should support the main idea.

Read each topic. Then write the most important point you want readers to know about
the topic.

1. Topic: Louisville, Kentucky little league players
The most important point about this topic: <u>won the Little League World Series</u>

2. Topic: Dogs
The most important point about this topic: _____

_____

3. Topic: Smoking
The most important point about this topic: _____

_____

4. Topic: My best friend
The most important point about this topic: _____

_____

5. Topic: My favorite birthday
The most important point about this topic: _____

_____

6. Topic: Video games
The most important point about this topic: _____

_____

0-7424-1804-9 *Building Grammar & Writing Skills*

Name _____ Date _____

Terrific Topics

A **paragraph** has a **topic sentence**. The key to writing a good paragraph is writing a good topic sentence. A topic sentence tells what the paragraph is about, and often includes the main idea. It is sometimes the first or second sentence in the paragraph.

Here is a simple formula for writing a topic sentence:

Topic
Running

+

A specific feeling or impression
helps people stay healthy

=

Topic Sentence
Running helps people
stay healthy.

Use the formula to write a topic sentence for each given topic.

1. Topic
My sister/
brother

+

A specific feeling or impression

=

Topic Sentence

2. Topic
My favorite
animal

+

A specific feeling or impression

=

Topic Sentence

3. Topic
Caring
for pets

+

A specific feeling or impression

=

Topic Sentence

4. Topic
My favorite
sport

+

A specific feeling or impression

=

Topic Sentence

5. Topic
TV
commercials

+

A specific feeling or impression

=

Topic Sentence

0-7424-1804-9 *Building Grammar & Writing Skills*

Name _____ Date _____

In Harmony

A **paragraph** has **supporting sentences**. Supporting sentences provide details that describe or support the main idea. This brings a sense of **unity** to the paragraph.

Read each paragraph. Circle the topic sentence. Cross out the sentence that is an unrelated idea.

1. Owning a pet is a major responsibility. All pets need food, water, a clean place to live, exercise, and lots of love. Some pets need more attention than others. Birds, gerbils, and hamsters can get exercise and entertain themselves with toys in their cages. I had a pet hamster, but it died. Dogs and cats rely on their owners to play with them. No matter what kind of pet it is, all pets require time. Before buying a pet, be sure you are able to meet all of the animal's needs.

2. On Friday, we will vote for our new school mascot. It will be fun to vote and exciting to watch the results. I will be cheering for the Cougars to win and enjoying the suspense if the vote is close. On Saturday, I am going to the watch our school football team play the Tigers. No matter what mascot wins, an election is a special and exciting occasion.

3. It is my mother's birthday. My Dad and I are throwing a surprise party for her. We cleaned the house, because the party will be at our house. We also baked my mom's favorite cake and decorated it with red roses. Last year, we took my mom out to eat for her birthday. Then we wrapped gifts and hid them under my bed. My aunt took my mom to the movies so we could get ready for the party and the guests can arrive and hide. When mom comes back, she will be so surprised!

4. The library is one of my favorite places in the world. It has books on every subject I like. I can read fiction, nonfiction, and poetry books. It also has numerous magazines I can read. I can spend hours at the library learning about many new things. My favorite author is Matt Christopher.

0-7424-1804-9 *Building Grammar & Writing Skills*

Name _____ Date _____

Make It Flow

Transition words are powerful tools for connecting **supporting sentences** in a paragraph. They help the sentences flow smoothly for the reader.

Example: Our dog, Gracie, intimidates people **because** she is very big and has a fierce bark. **However**, she is really as gentle as a kitten. **Therefore**, she is useful but harmless.

Rewrite each paragraph. Use transition words so it flows more smoothly.
Hint: You can combine sentences. Here are some transition words you can use: *when, however, until, as a result, consequently, while, thus, because, and, meanwhile, therefore.*

1. I use to be an only child. My parents had my two brothers. Now my life is chaos. My brothers constantly run around, yell, scream, and get into trouble.

_____

_____

_____

2. My older brother, Jacob, constantly teases me. My younger brother, Logan, always uses my crayons without my permission. He breaks them. I love them both.

_____

_____

3. Floppy, our rabbit, escaped from her pen. We tried to catch her. She hopped away from us. We had to try something else. I dangled a carrot to get her attention. My brother sneaked up behind her. The moment he was about to grab her, she hopped away. My brother landed flat on his face.

_____

_____

_____

_____

75

Name _____ Date _____

Silly Sequences

A **paragraph** has supporting sentences. **Supporting sentences** provide details that describe or support the main idea. They are arranged in a logical, natural order.

Supporting sentences are arranged in **sequential order** if the writer is describing a series of events or specific instructions.

Each paragraph below has a topic and closing sentence. However, the supporting sentences are out of order. Number the sentences in the proper order. Then rewrite the paragraphs on a separate sheet of paper.

I. It was my birthday, and I couldn't wait for the day to begin. ☐ After breakfast, I brushed my teeth, washed my face, and combed my hair. ☐ My mom was surprised to see me because she usually has to call me several times to get up and get ready. ☐ Finally, I hugged my mom good-bye and ran out the door. ☐ As soon as I woke up, I jumped out of bed and made it. ☐ Next, I ran back downstairs and grabbed my lunch and backpack. ☐ Then I quickly got dressed and ran downstairs to the kitchen for breakfast. It was going to be an awesome day!

2. Dogs help people in many ways. ☐ In addition, dogs guide blind people and serve as "ears" for people who are deaf. ☐ Furthermore, they lift the spirits of patients in hospitals and nursing homes. ☐ For example, dogs help police officers track criminals, find missing children, and sniff out illegal drugs. These are only a few of the many ways that dogs help people.

0-7424-1804-9 *Building Grammar & Writing Skills*

Name _____ Date _____

Cats and Dogs

In a **compare and contrast** paragraph, the **supporting sentences** describe or explain the similarities and/or differences between two or more people, places, things, or ideas.

When writing supporting sentences, the following **transition word**s may be used so that your paragraph flows smoothly and has unity and rhythm.

Similarities	Differences
is similar to	on the other hand
both	however
also	but
too	in contrast
as well	differs from
	while
	unlike

Compare a cat and a dog.
List three ways they are alike.

_____

_____

_____

Using your lists, write a paragraph about how cats and dogs are alike and different. Use at least four transition words in your paragraph.

_____

_____

_____

_____

_____

_____

0-7424-1804-9 *Building Grammar & Writing Skills*

Name _____ Date _____

  # *Wrapping It Up*

The **closing sentence** is the last sentence in a **paragraph**. To write a closing sentence, restate the main idea using different words, write a conclusive statement, or write a question relating to the topic and main idea. Try to avoid using words such as in conclusion, in summary.

Read each paragraph. Then write an appropriate closing sentence.

1.   My birthday is the best day of the year. My parents always have a party for me. All my friends come over and bring gifts. We eat cake and ice cream. We also play games, and everyone gets prizes.

_____

2.   The second largest river in the United States is the Mississippi. This river is sometimes called "Old Man River." The source of the river is in northwestern Minnesota. The Mississippi River travels 2,340 miles south to the Gulf of Mexico. It helps form the borders of ten states. It is our nation's chief inland waterway. Ships travel the river carrying agricultural goods, industrial products, and raw materials.

_____

3.   Owls are nocturnal animals. They sleep during the day and hunt at night. In the dark, they silently swoop down on their prey. Their feathers muffle the swishing sound that most birds make when they fly. They have been called the "night watchman of our gardens," because they catch and eat harmful rodents after dark. Although owls have keen night vision, some have such sensitive hearing that they rely very little on sight. Rather, these owls locate and catch their prey in total darkness by listening to the rustling noises they make.

_____

4.   In order to become good pets, it is important for puppies to have contact with people. Newborn puppies should be handled gently for a few minutes each day. They need even more contact when they are four to ten weeks old. If puppies do not get human contact, they may become aggressive. If you are going to adopt a puppy, it is best to do so when it is six to eight weeks old.

_____

78

Name _____ Date _____

A Perfect Paragraph

Remember, a paragraph has:
- one main idea
- a topic sentence
- supporting sentences that
    - describe or support the main idea
    - are related to the topic sentence
    - are arranged in a logical, natural order
- a closing sentence

Use this graphic organizer to organize your ideas for a paragraph. Then write your paragraph on a separate sheet of paper.

My Topic

↓

My Main Idea

↓

My Topic Sentence

↓

My Supporting Details

↓

My Concluding Sentence

79

Name _____ Date _____

Writing a Multiple-Paragraph Essay

Every **essay** is made up of three parts:

Introduction
The introductory paragraph

This paragraph does two things:
- Briefly tells the reader about the topic and main idea of your essay
- Catches the reader's interest. You can:
  - Begin with a question.
  - Begin with an amusing or interesting story about your topic.
  - Begin with a quotation.
  - Begin with a startling statement.

Body
The **body** follows the introduction. It consists of a number of supporting paragraphs in which you develop your ideas in detail.

Each paragraph includes:
- A topic sentence introducing your main point for the paragraph
- Details, facts, and quotations to support the main point of the paragraph
- An example to support the main point of the paragraph
- Transitional words to make the sentences flow smoothly

Conclusion
The concluding paragraph

This paragraph summarizes the main points of the supporting paragraphs, leaving out specific examples.
- Reemphasize the main idea of your essay.
- Refer back to your attention-getting device from the introductory paragraph.

0-7424-1804-9 *Building Grammar & Writing Skills*

Name _____ Date _____

What an Introduction!

An **introductory paragraph** does two things. It catches the interest of the reader and briefly tells about the topic and main idea.

One way to begin an introductory paragraph is to ask and then answer a question. The answer should include details that interest and introduce the reader to the topic.

Example: What's so great about running? Well, everything—running builds stronger bones, increases our brainpower, may help prevent Alzheimer's disease, and other additional benefits. So grab your running shoes, and let's start running today.

Another way to introduce a topic is to begin with an anecdote. An **anecdote** is an amusing or interesting story about your topic.

Example: When I came home from school yesterday, I called to my mom. No one answered. Suddenly I heard heavy breathing and the pounding of steps rapidly approaching me from behind. Before I could turn around a big furry creature pounced on me, knocking me to the ground and licking my face uncontrollably. It was the puppy I had always wanted, and my parents had bought him for my ninth birthday!

Choose one of the following topics or choose your own. Then write an introductory paragraph below. Use either the question-and-answer style or an anecdote.

Topics

The Most Important Person in My Life   **Destruction of the Rain Forest**
The Day I Was Invisible   **A Memorable Present**

Topic: _____

_____

_____

_____

_____

_____

_____

0-7424-1804-9 *Building Grammar & Writing Skills*

Name _____ Date _____

Outlaw Run-ons

A **run-on sentence** is two or more sentences (independent clauses) that run together without correct punctuation. One way to correct a run-on sentence is to add a period to separate the two sentences. Eliminating run-on sentences from your writing will make your thoughts easier to follow and understand.

Example: Maria and John like skiing Karen does not. (run-on)
Maria and John like skiing. Karen does not. (two sentences)

Read the sentences aloud to find where to separate the run-on sentence into two complete sentences. When reading aloud, you naturally pause at the end of a sentence. Use these proofreading marks to correct the run-on sentences.

m̲̲̲   Capitalize (Underline three times letters that should be capitalized.)

⊙   Insert period

1. This is not such a wonderful playground still, the kids like it.

2. Those swings are the ones Dina always chooses they are just her size.

3. Because the weather is so hot, we changed our plans we will go to the beach tomorrow.

4. The papers were all messed up therefore, we couldn't find the report we needed.

5. We have an idea the city council should consider it might solve the city's problems.

6. My report on whales is due tomorrow I have to type the report tonight.

7. These game rules are puzzling to me I refuse to play until you explain them.

8. Since Darren defended us, the bullies have left us alone they must respect Darren's reputation.

9. I saw hummingbirds around that tree yesterday I think they have been nesting look to see if you can see them.

10. This suntan lotion will protect you from the sun try it before you get sunburned.

0-7424-1804-9 *Building Grammar & Writing Skills*

Name _____ Date _____

Easy Elaboration

One way to expand simple sentences is to **elaborate** using adjectives and adverbs. To elaborate, add one or two adjectives to describe the noun and ask yourself *who, what, where, when, why,* and *how.* Then incorporate your answers into a simple sentence.

Answer each question. Then rewrite the simple sentence using your answers. The first one is done for you.

1. I like ice cream.

What kind? mint chocolate chip	**Where?** from Stanley's Ice Cream Parlor	**When?** after playing baseball

New Sentence: I like mint chocolate-chip ice cream from Stanley's Ice Cream Parlor after playing baseball.

2. The band played.

How? **Why?** **When?**

_____

3. The fox jumped.

What kind? **How?** **Why?**

_____

4. The car crashed.

What kind? **Where?** **When?**

_____

5. The girl ran.

Why? **Where?** **When?**

_____

0-7424-1804-9 *Building Grammar & Writing Skills*

Name _____ Date _____

Good Choices

A **thesaurus** is a book that contains synonyms and antonyms of words. Many words have very slight differences in their meanings. By choosing words carefully, a writer can create a clearer image for a reader.

Read each sentence. Then use a thesaurus to find a word to replace the boldfaced word. Rewrite the sentence using your new word.

1. This apple pie is **good**.

   _____

2. Justin **cried** when he slammed the car door on his finger.

   _____

3. The mouse **ran** when she saw the cat.

   _____

4. Mr. Smith **asked** about the price of the house.

   _____

5. The elephant **walked** over to the watering hole.

   _____

6. The kitchen is **messy** after my dad cooks.

   _____

7. It was a **disaster** when the tornado hit and ruined all those houses.

   _____

8. Jerome **jumped** out of his seat when he heard the loud boom.

   _____

9. Henry was **happy** when he got a horse for his birthday.

   _____

10. Keisha painted her picture with **pretty** colors.

    _____

0-7424-1804-9 *Building Grammar & Writing Skills*

Name _____ Date _____

Sly as a Fox

A **simile** is a comparison of similar things using the words *like* or *as*. A writer can create a clearer image for the reader by using similes.

Write a simile to complete each sentence. The first one is done for you.

1. Our dog is as large as <u>a horse</u>.

2. Victoria's hair is as red as _____.

3. That baby waddles like _____.

4. My grandfather's feet were as big as _____.

5. My dad's snoring sounds like _____ stampeding through the house.

6. The useless football player was as clumsy as _____.

7. As fast as _____, Scott ran to the finish line.

8. My grandmother's hands were like _____ from working in the fields.

9. The clouds were fluffy like _____.

Use each noun to write a simile. Remember to compare the noun to another noun that will create a picture in the reader's mind. Use the words *like* or *as*.

10. monster's eyes _____

11. Chelsea's smile _____

12. car _____

13. boy _____

14. oatmeal cookies _____

0-7424-1804-9 *Building Grammar & Writing Skills*

Name _____ Date _____

He's a Monster

A **metaphor** is a direct comparison, without using the words *like* or *as*. A metaphor often uses verbs such as *is*, *are*, *was*, or *were*. Writers use metaphors to make their writing more interesting or entertaining.

Write appropriate metaphors from the list to complete the sentences.

1. The car salesperson was _____.

2. Hayley was _____, blocking every volleyball as it came over the net.

3. The moon is _____, floating in the sky.

4. The basketball fans were _____, erupting each time their team scored.

5. The smoke from the forest fire was _____, covering the valley.

6. Mr. McPhearson, _____, won the marathon and broke last year's record.

> **Metaphors**
> explosive volcanoes
> a balloon
> a thick blanket
> a bolt of lightning
> a fierce shark
> a wall

Compare each noun to another noun by writing your own metaphor. The first one is done for you.

7. umbrella   Compared to: <u>roof</u>
   <u>The umbrella was a roof over my head.</u>

8. tornado   Compared to: _____

   _____

9. ocean   Compared to: _____

   _____

10. elephant   Compared to: _____

   _____

0-7424-1804-9 *Building Grammar & Writing Skills*

Name _____ Date _____

It's All in the Almanac

An **almanac** contains thousands of facts and figures on virtually every topic—from the government to the Internet to sports. The **table of contents** shows the major divisions in a book. It comes right before the book's body and is used to help locate major topics or areas.

Table of Contents

Astronomy and Calendar	..275	World Exploration and Geography	...586
Awards, Medals, Prizes	...316	Health	.608
Noted Personalities	333	Associations and Societies	621
United States Populations	..376	Postal Information	633
Language	439	Science and Technology	638
Presidential Elections	446	Computers	643
Flags and Maps	481	United States Cities.	693
United States History	540	Buildings, Bridges, Tunnels	703
World History	551	Consumer Information	720
Historical Figures	577	Sports	849

Use the Table of Contents to answer each question.

1. On what page does "Flags and Maps" begin? _____

2. You are mailing a package to Madison, Wisconsin, but you don't know the zip code. Under which section would you look? _____

3. You want to find the population of the state of Alabama. Under which section would you look? _____

4. On what page does "World History" end? _____

5. You want to find out who won the World Series in baseball. Under which section would you look? _____

6. You want to find out who were the Newbery Medal winners in 1995 and 1999. Under which section and page number would you look? _____
_____

7. You want to find facts about Akron, Ohio. Under which section would you look?
_____

8. Which section begins on page 446? _____

0-7424-1804-9 *Building Grammar & Writing Skills*

Name _____ Date _____

Amazing Almanac

An **almanac** contains thousands of facts and figures on virtually every topic—from the government to the Internet to Sports.

Use an almanac to locate the following information.

1. Write the name of the state where you live: _____

2. List four current facts about your state. List the section title and page number on which you found the information.

Fact 2: _____
_____
_____
_____
_____

Section: _____

Page: _____

Fact 2: _____
_____
_____
_____
_____

Section: _____ Page: _____

Fact 2: _____
_____
_____
_____

Section: _____ Page: _____

0-7424-1804-9 *Building Grammar & Writing Skills*

Name _____ Date _____

Guide Words

In a **dictionary**, a pair of **guide words** is printed at the top of each page. The entries that fall alphabetically between the guide words are found on that page. The first guide word is the first entry on the page. The second guide word is the last entry on the page.

Fill in the circle of the page (guide words) where you would find each word.

1. earthmover
- O e • earphone
- O ear pick • eastern
- O easterner • echelle
- O echelon • economy

2. bumblebee
- O bud • buggy
- O bughouse • bulletin
- O bulletin • buncos
- O bund • burgess

3. lunar
- O luminaria • lupus erthematosus
- O lurch • luxuriantly
- O luxuriate • lyonnaise
- O Lyonnesse • Maccabees

4. okapi
- O offer • offstage
- O off-the-books • old
- O old • olfactory
- O olfactory bulb • omitting

5. player
- O plastic • platitudinously
- O platonic • player
- O player piano • pleio
- O pleiotropic • plisse

6. disinterested
- O disbursement • discomfort
- O discomfort • discreet
- O discreetly • disgrace
- O disgraceful • disinterestedly

7. tabby
- O systematic • tableful
- O table-hop • tactfulness
- O tactic • tailor
- O tailorbird • take a powder

8. canceled
- O Cambodian • campy
- O campylobacter • candidature
- O candid-camera • cannonade
- O cannonball • canthus

9. appreciative
- O apologetically • apparatus
- O apparel • application
- O applicative • approved
- O approved • school arabesque

0-7424-1804-9 *Building Grammar & Writing Skills*

Name _____ Date _____

Encyclopedia Search

You can use an **encyclopedia** to find factual information on a variety of topics. It is organized in alphabetical order by subject. If you are trying to find a person, look under the first letter of the person's last name.

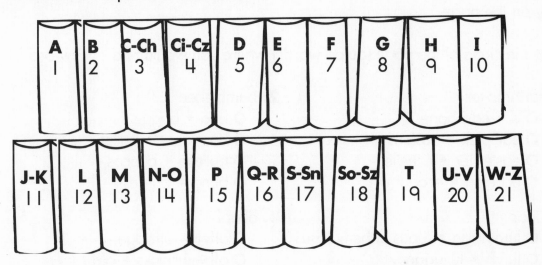

Write the volume of the encyclopedia in which you would find the following subjects.

1. birds Volume 2 B _____

2. Vikings _____

3. cardinal _____

4. solar system _____

5. cello _____

6. Henry Ford _____

7. constellation _____

8. silverfish _____

9. black widow _____

10. jack rabbit _____

11. Emily Dickinson _____

12. U.S. Government _____

13. spiders _____

14. Johnny Appleseed _____

15. Olympic Games _____

16. San Diego _____

17. gorilla _____

18. Mars _____

19. xylophone _____

20. George Washington _____

21. racquetball _____

22. Revolutionary War _____

0-7424-1804-9 *Building Grammar & Writing Skills*

Name _____ Date _____

At the Library

A card catalog is an index of nearly all the materials in the library. Books, for example, are listed in the card catalog by subject, author, and title. The cards are arranged in alphabetical order and filed in drawers.

These are subject cards:

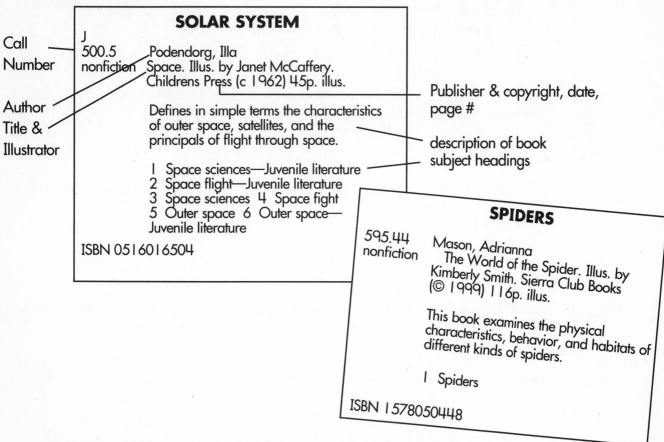

Call Number

Author

Title & Illustrator

SOLAR SYSTEM

J
500.5
nonfiction

Podendorg, Illa
Space. Illus. by Janet McCaffery.
Childrens Press (c 1962) 45p. illus.

Defines in simple terms the characteristics of outer space, satellites, and the principals of flight through space.

1 Space sciences—Juvenile literature
2 Space flight—Juvenile literature
3 Space sciences 4 Space fight
5 Outer space 6 Outer space—
Juvenile literature

ISBN 0516016504

Publisher & copyright, date, page #

description of book
subject headings

SPIDERS

595.44
nonfiction

Mason, Adrianna
The World of the Spider. Illus. by Kimberly Smith. Sierra Club Books (© 1999) 116p. illus.

This book examines the physical characteristics, behavior, and habitats of different kinds of spiders.

1 Spiders

ISBN 1578050448

Look at the spiders subject card above to fill in the following information.

Title: _____ Author: _____

Publisher: _____ Call No.: _____

Copyright Date: _____ Illustrator: _____

Summary: _____

_____

No. of Pages: _____

91

Name _____ Date _____

Show Me

Good writers don't just tell—they show. Writers **show** what a reader should see, what a character feels, and what happens by using descriptive words and phrases.

Example: The happy baby laughed. *(tell)*
Mia grabbed her pink teddy bear, giggling and squealing. Her belly shook and her legs kicked. *(show)*

Read each "telling" sentence. Then close your eyes and picture what you would see. Rewrite the sentence, *showing* the reader what he or she should see.

1. The bedroom was messy.

_____

2. The princess was pretty.

_____

Read each "telling" sentence. Then close your eyes, picture the character, and imagine what he or she feels. Rewrite the sentence, *showing* how the character feels.

3. Charlotte was happy.

_____

4. Mom was mad.

_____

Read each "telling" sentence. Then close your eyes and picture the action. Rewrite the sentence, *showing* the action.

5. Dad yelled at the dog.

_____

6. The teacher spoke to the class.

_____

0-7424-1804-9 *Building Grammar & Writing Skills*

Name _____ Date _____

Taking Notes

★ ★ ★ ★ ★ ★ ★

When you **take notes**, write down only the most important information—main idea and important details. Do not write complete sentences. Notes are brief and to the point.

Read this informational article. Then take notes on another paper by writing the main idea and important details below.

The Three Branches of Government

The writers of the United States Constitution wanted to create a strong national government. However, they also wanted to make sure that one person or group did not have too much power. That is why they created the three branches of government—legislative, executive, and judicial.

Congress makes up the legislative branch. Congress consists of two chambers—the Senate and the House of Representatives. The main job of Congress is making our nation's laws. Other powers include collecting and spending money from taxes and declaring war.

The executive branch enforces the federal laws. The president is the head of the executive branch. The vice-president and cabinet members are also part of the executive branch. The president appoints the cabinet members, who head the 14 major departments of the government. Cabinet members advise the president. The president signs and enforces laws. Other powers include serving as the head of our armed forces and making treaties with other nations. However, the Senate must approve all treaties.

The judicial branch is made up of numerous federal courts and judges. The judicial branch interprets our nation's laws. The Supreme Court of the United States is the highest court in our nation.

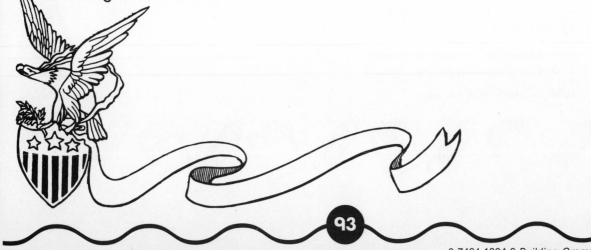

0-7424-1804-9 *Building Grammar & Writing Skills*

Name _____ Date _____

Editing Checklist

Proofreading Marks

Jen∧   Insert word

∧   Add a comma

Jen   Add quotation marks

Jen's   Add apostrophe

Jen   Delete

∧·   Add period

JEn   Lowercase

jen   Capitalize

New paragraph

(stet)   Let it stand

(sp)   Spelling

Make sure you:

Capitalize the title.
Punctuate the title.
  • Titles of long works are underlined.
  • Titles of short works are in quotation marks.
Capitalize the first word in each sentence.
Capitalize proper nouns.
Indent paragraphs.
Use quotation marks and commas with direct quotes.
Use complete sentences.
Use the proper punctuation mark at the ends of sentences. (. ? !)
Use apostrophes in contractions.
Use apostrophes in possessive nouns.
Use commas in a series.
Use apostrophes in possessive nouns.
Use transitional words.
Use descriptive words.

0-7424-1804-9 *Building Grammar & Writing Skills*

Name _____ Date _____

How Do You Do That?

A **how-to paragraph** is an example of **expository writing**. It tells what materials will be needed and gives step-by-step instructions on how to do something.

Write a how-to paragraph. Choose from one of the topics below, or choose your own. Remember to use sequencing words such as *first, next, then,* and *last.*

Topics

How to make an ice cream sundae   How to tie your shoe

How to make a pizza   How to build a campfire

How to brush your teeth   How to make a bed

_____

_____

_____

_____

_____

_____

_____

_____

_____

_____

_____

       0-7424-1804-9 *Building Grammar & Writing Skills*

Name _____ Date _____

Wonderful Women

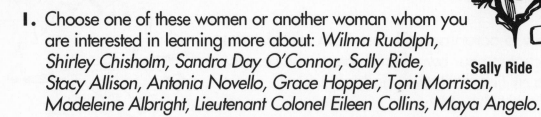

A **biographical sketch** tells the story of another person's life. It focuses on one incident that tells about who he or she is.

Sally Ride

1. Choose one of these women or another woman whom you are interested in learning more about: *Wilma Rudolph, Shirley Chisholm, Sandra Day O'Connor, Sally Ride, Stacy Allison, Antonia Novello, Grace Hopper, Toni Morrison, Madeleine Albright, Lieutenant Colonel Eileen Collins, Maya Angelo.*

2. Brainstorm a list of questions to ask about this person. List your questions in the chart below. Some sample questions include: *Where and when was this person born? Where did she grow up? What does or did she do for a living? Why is she famous? What does or did she do to become famous? How has she made an impact on others' lives?*

3. Research to gather facts and answers to your questions. Use various sources, such as books, encyclopedias, the Internet, newspapers, and magazines. Write your answers and the sources you used in the chart.

4. Review your notes and choose one important thing you discovered about this person. Research this idea further.

5. Create an outline.

6. On a separate sheet of paper, write your biographical sketch. Describe this person using facts and events. You also might to try using quotes.

Questions	Answers	Sources

0-7424-1804-9 *Building Grammar & Writing Skills*

Name _____ Date _____

Black History Month

A **biographical sketch** tells the story of another person's life. It focuses on one incident that tells about who he or she is.

1. Choose one of these people or another African American whom you are interested in learning more about: *Frederick Douglass, Jackie Robinson, Louis Armstrong, Jesse Owens, Colin Powell, Thurgood Marshall, Rosa Parks, Harriet Tubman, Ida B. Wells-Barnett, Marian Anderson, Mary Elizabeth Bowser, Sojourner Truth, Florence Griffith-Joyner, Alice Walker, Medgar Evers.*

2. Brainstorm a list of questions to ask about this person. List your questions in the chart below. Some sample questions include: *Where and when was this person born? Where did this person grow up? What does or did this person do for a living? Why is this person famous? What does or did this person do to become famous? How has this person made an impact on others' lives?*

3. Research to gather facts and answers to your questions. Use various sources, such as books, encyclopedias, the Internet, newspapers, and magazines. Write your answers and the sources you used in the chart.

4. Review your notes and choose one important thing you discovered about this person. Research this idea further.

5. Create an outline.

Frederick Douglass

6. On a separate sheet of paper, write your biographical sketch. Describe this person using facts and events. You also might try using quotes.

Questions	Answers	Sources

97

 0-7424-1804-9 *Building Grammar & Writing Skills*

Name _____ Date _____

My Life

An **autobiography** is the story of your life—that you write yourself!

Think about your life. Brainstorm a list of major events on a separate sheet of paper, such as the birth of siblings, meeting your best friend, moving to a new city, getting a pet, or winning an award.

Next, choose three events besides your birth, and list them in sequential order below. Write five details about each event.

Finally, use this information to write your autobiography.

Event: Birth

_____

_____

_____

_____

_____

Event: _____ **Age:** ____

_____

_____

_____

_____

_____

Event: _____ **Age:** ___   **Event:** _____ **Age:** ___

_____   _____

_____   _____

_____   _____

_____   _____

_____   _____

0-7424-1804-9 *Building Grammar & Writing Skills*

Name _____ Date _____

All About Boa Constrictors

You are writing a short article about boa constrictors for the local zoo newsletter. You have gathered the following facts about boa constrictors. Use these facts to write your article. Remember to use an introductory sentence that grabs the reader's attention.

- closely related to the python
- pale sandy brown color, 15 to 20 brown marks on its back
- normally grows 10 feet long
- largest ever caught was 18.5 feet long
- native to the tropical forests of Central and South America
- may find it in trees, but mostly on the ground
- lives in hollow logs, mammal burrows
- eats birds, iguanas, and monkeys
- has a keen sense of smell used to detect other animals
- kills its prey by coiling around and suffocating
- hinged jaws enable it to swallow animals
- will hiss and strike when provoked
- can be easily tamed and maintained in zoos

Title: _____

_____
_____
_____
_____
_____
_____
_____
_____
_____

0-7424-1804-9 *Building Grammar & Writing Skills*

Name _____ Date _____

Everyday Gadgets

Think of something you use every day and would like to learn more about, such as a fork, can opener, toilet, pencil, telephone, sticky notepads, or Velcro. Use various resources to find the answers to the following questions. Then write each answer and list the source. Finally, use this information to write an informative report on a separate sheet of paper.

Object: _____

Who invented it? _____

Source: _____

More details about the inventor:

_____

Source: _____

When was it invented? _____

Source: _____

Why was it invented? _____

Source: _____

How did the inventor come up with the idea? _____

Source: _____

Other facts you would like to know. _____

_____

0-7424-1804-9 *Building Grammar & Writing Skills*

Name _____ Date _____

Extra! Extra! Read All About It!

You are a newspaper reporter. You are writing a report on an extracurricular event taking place at your school. Use the outline below to gather your information.

1. Who is presenting the event? _____

2. What is the event? _____

3. Where will the event take place? _____

4. What are the event (date(s) and time(s)? _____

5. What is the cost? _____

6. Why is the school having this event? _____
_____

7. Other details or information: _____
_____

Use the following format to write your newspaper article. Write your article on a separate sheet of paper.

Parts of a News Article
Headline: Title that will catch the reader's interest
Lead: Introduces the story; usually contains one or two sentences that include the most important details.
Body: Main part of the news article that provides the rest of the details; the most important details come first.

Headline
Lead:_____
_____
Body:_____
_____
_____

0-7424-1804-9 *Building Grammar & Writing Skills*

Name _____ Date _____

In My Opinion

Choose one of the following topics, or choose one you feel
strongly about. Then write your opinion and supporting reasons.

Topics
Should schools ban serving or offering sodas in school?
Should bike riders, skateboarders, and rollerbladers wear helmets?
Should physical education be eliminated from the curriculum?
Should my bedtime be at 10 o'clock on weeknights?

Topic: _____

In my opinion,_____

_____

_____

Three reasons supporting my opinion and an example or detail to support each reason:

Reason 1: _____
Example or detail: _____

_____

Reason 2: _____
Example or detail: _____

_____

Reason 3: _____
Example or detail: _____

_____

My final persuasive ending statement: _____

_____

Using these ideas, write a short paragraph persuading others to support your opinion.

0-7424-1804-9 *Building Grammar & Writing Skills*

Name _____ Date _____

Join the Club

Think about a club, sport, or activity in which you enjoy participating. What would you say to persuade other students to join your club? Write an article for your school newspaper, urging students to participate in the club, sport, or activity that you believe would be enjoyable for them.

Use this graphic organizer to plan your article.

My Audience:

↓

My Point of View:

↓

How I can grab the reader's attention in the first paragraph:

↓

Three reasons, facts, or examples to support my point of view:
_____
_____
_____

↓

Final sentences urging students to join:
_____
_____
_____
_____

Using these ideas, write your article on a separate sheet of paper.

103

 0-7424-1804-9 *Building Grammar & Writing Skills*

Name _____ Date _____

Litter Letter

Litter has become a problem at your school. Students are throwing trash on the playground and leaving empty bottles and cans on benches. Also, students are leaving trash on the cafeteria tables rather than throwing it away. They are littering the cafeteria floor with paper bags, napkins, and other trash. Your principal has asked students to be responsible and clean up after themselves, but there is still litter everywhere. Now, the principal has banned all playground activities until the problem is fixed. What is your position on this issue?

Write a letter to your principal. In the first paragraph, state why you are writing the letter, state your position, and support it with details. In the second paragraph, suggest an alternative solution to the problem and persuade him or her to try it.

Date: _____

Dear _____,

_____

_____

_____

_____

_____

_____

_____

_____

Sincerely,

_____

104

Name _____ Date _____

Dear Ms. Blume . . .

Who is your favorite author? Write a letter to this person.
Use the questions below to plan your letter.

Name two reasons why you like this author's books and an
example to support each reason.

Reason 1: _____

Example: _____

_____

Reason 2: _____

Example: _____

_____

What is your favorite book by this author? _____

Name two reasons why you liked this book and an example to support each reason.

Reason 1: _____

Example: _____

_____

Reason 2: _____

Example: _____

_____

Who is your favorite character? _____

Why is he/she your favorite character? _____

_____

Write three questions you would like to ask this author.

1. _____
2. _____
3. _____

0-7424-1804-9 *Building Grammar & Writing Skills*

Name _____ Date _____

At the Movies

You are a famous movie critic for the local newspaper. Choose a movie you've seen recently, and write a movie review for it. Remember to include: title, main characters, summary, and why you liked the movie, supporting your reasons with specific examples. Give it a rating (1–5 stars, with 5 being the best).

Example: *Spy Kids*—A glorified gizmo movie, but the gizmos have a loopy, crazy energy. The story, about a brother and sister who become entwined in the surreal adventure of their secret-agent parents, is flip, airy, and fun. You can feel the delight director Robert Rodriguez took in layering on the special effects. The parents make a winning pair, but it's the elf who takes over the movie—the impish Fegan Floop; he's the world's naughtiest elf! Rating: ★★★

_____
_____
_____
_____
_____
_____
_____
_____
_____
_____

Rating:

0-7424-1804-9 *Building Grammar & Writing Skills*

Name _____ Date _____

About a Book

You work for a children's publishing company. Your assignment is to write a summary of a book that will appear on the book jacket. Choose a book that you recently finished reading. To plan your summary, complete the information below.

Title: _____

Author: _____

Setting (time and place): _____

Main character(s): _____

Theme (main idea of the story): _____
_____

Plot (What is the story mostly about? What is the main event or conflict? What events lead up to it? What happens as a result?) _____
_____
_____

Why should people read this book? _____
_____
_____

Write your book summary below:
_____
_____
_____
_____
_____

0-7424-1804-9 *Building Grammar & Writing Skills*

Name _____ Date _____

Special Surprise

A **personal narrative** is a real-life story about you. It tells about an experience in an informative and entertaining way. You are the main character.

Think about a time when you received a special gift or something unexpected. It could be a birthday gift or an unexpected card, treat, or reward. Answer the questions to help you plan your narrative. Then write your narrative on a separate sheet of paper.

1. What was the gift? Describe it. _____

_____

2. Who gave you this gift? _____

3. When did you get this gift? _____

4. What was the time of year? _____

5. Why did you get this gift? _____

_____

6. Where were you when you received this gift? _____

_____

7. Were there other people around? Who? _____

_____

8. How did you feel after you got the gift?

_____

9. What made this gift so special? _____

_____

10. What other details can you think of to describe the experience (sights, smells, tastes, sounds, feelings)? _____

_____

108

Name _____ Date _____

Memorable Moment

A **personal narrative** is a real-life story about *you*. It tells about an experience in an informative and entertaining way. You are the main character.

Think about a time when you were happy, sad, or scared. Write a story about this moment in your life. Narrate the event or series of events. Use descriptions that help the reader see, hear, smell, or taste what is going on. Include your thoughts and feelings, and use dialogue. (Continue on another sheet of paper if you need more room.)

_____

_____

_____

_____

_____

_____

_____

_____

_____

_____

_____

_____

0-7424-1804-9 *Building Grammar & Writing Skills*

Name _____ Date _____

Where Do You Shop?

Realistic fiction is a story that *could* be true, but it isn't. Realistic fiction can also include some facts that are true. It has two main purposes—to tell an interesting story and to send an important message (theme).

Use the story starter below to write a realistic fiction story. Read the information. Think about events or actions that might lead to a solution. Fill in the boxes. Then write your story on a separate sheet of paper.

Setting: School	**Main Characters:** Fourth graders: Alex, Callie, Maria, Tham
Theme:	**Problem:** Tham, Alex, Callie, and Maria are all classmates. Maria and Tham always tease Callie because of the clothes she wears. Alex overhears them teasing her.

Event:

Event:

Event:

Solution:

0-7424-1804-9 *Building Grammar & Writing Skills*

King Alfonzo

A **fairy tale** usually consists of the following elements:
Characters—good and bad
Setting
Magical Element
Problem
Solution/Reward
Ending: *They lived happily ever after!*

Below is the beginning of a fairy tale. Identify the characters, setting, and problem. Think of other characters, a magical element, and a solution/reward. Then complete the fairy tale.

Once upon a time, King Alfonzo and Queen Jasmine lived in a beautiful castle at the top of the hill, overlooking the kingdom. Everyone in the kingdom loved the king and queen, for they were the kindest, happiest people who ever ruled.

One day, King Alfonzo went out for his daily ride and encountered a wicked witch. When he returned to the castle, he was mean, grumpy, and miserable. Now, all King Alfonzo does is sit on his throne and shout, "I am the king! You must do as I say!"

_____

_____

_____

_____

_____

_____

_____

_____

Name _____ Date _____

I'm Not a Big, Bad Wolf!

Pretend you are the wolf from the *Three Little Pigs.* Finish writing the story from the wolf's viewpoint.

    One day I was feeling very sad and lonely, because my best friend moved away and I didn't have anyone to play with. My mother told me that I would have to go out and make some new friends. So I walked around for a very long time, but I couldn't find anyone! Finally, I came to a house made out of straw. I thought perhaps there was someone inside who might want to play, so I knocked on the door.

_____

_____

_____

_____

_____

_____

_____

_____

_____

_____

_____

_____

_____

_____

0-7424-1804-9 *Building Grammar & Writing Skills*

Name _____ Date _____

Too Tall Tale

A **tall tale** is a story about someone who did something incredible, which has been handed down through history. As the story is retold, its events become more and more exaggerated. A tall tale may have a factual basis, but many of its parts are not true.

1. Choose a tall tale hero. Think of someone who is strong, smart, brave, or athletic.
2. Exaggerate your hero's characteristics. Make him or her bigger or stronger or faster or smarter than anyone else.
3. Create an adventure for your hero. Once again, exaggerate! The events cannot happen in real life.
4. Use the story plan below to help you write your own tall tale.

(Your hero's name) was the (adjectives describing your hero) man/woman/ animal in the state of (name your state). He/She was (use a metaphor or simile about your hero's bravery, strength, or intelligence), and could (describe some amazing, incredible things your hero can do). Everyone in the state knew (hero's name) and loved to tell and retell his/her amazing feats.

One time (hero's name) went to visit (second character's name). (Second character's name) had been having tremendous problems with (make up some problems for your hero to solve for his/her friend). (Second character's name) explained his/her problem to (hero's name). "Say no more," said (hero's name). Immediately, he/she (explain how your hero solved the problem). (Second character's name) was so excited and relieved that he/she (explain what he/she did to thank your hero).

0-7424-1804-9 *Building Grammar & Writing Skills*

Name _____ Date _____

Why the Sky Is Blue

Myths are make-believe stories that explain how things came to be. They usually tell about the creation of mythical gods or elements of nature. Most cultures past and present have myths that are passed down from generation to generation.

Choose one of these topics, or use your own idea. Write a myth about it.

Topics

Why leopards have spots	**Why the earth is round**
How lightning came to be	**Why ducks can float**
Why elephants have trunks	**Why volcanoes erupt**
Why there are earthquakes	**How the mountains were formed**
Why the moon comes out at night	**Why the sky is blue**

Title: _____

A long time ago, _____

_____

_____

_____

_____

_____

_____

And that is why _____ .

114

Name _____ Date _____

The Moral of the Story

A **fable** is a short story used to teach a lesson. This lesson is called a **moral**. The moral is written at the end of the fable. The characters are usually animals that speak and act like humans.

Use this story plan to help you write a fable. Then write your fable on a separate sheet of paper.

1. Write a lesson that you have learned.

_____

2. What happened that helped you learn this lesson? What was the problem?

_____

3. Write two kinds of animals and give them names.

_____   _____

_____   _____

4. Choose one of the animals to be the main character—the one that learns the lesson (label him/her #1). Choose the other animal to be the supporting character—the one who helps the main character learn the lesson (label him/her #2).

5. Describe something the main character is doing to cause the problem.

_____

6. Think of a problem or situation the supporting character can create to teach the lesson to the main character. _____

_____

7. Describe how this new problem affects the main character. _____

_____

8. Finally, describe how the supporting character reveals the lesson to the main character. _____

_____

115

Name _____ Date _____

Pooh Bear's Adventure

Pooh Bear, a 13-year-old Pomeranian, disappeared from her home in Florida. Her owner put up fliers and called every shelter in town, but could not find Pooh Bear anywhere! Six years later, Pooh Bear's owner received a call from a vet in Cincinnati, Ohio, who scanned Pooh Bear's lost-pet microchip and found her number. How she wound up at a marina on the Ohio River remains a mystery. Of course, Pooh Bear is not talking!

Pretend you are Pooh Bear. Use a map to plot Pooh Bear's adventure. How did Pooh Bear leave home? Where did she go first? Second? Next? Last? How did she get from one place to the next? What did she do in each place? Who did she meet? What problems did she face? Write a story about your adventures below.

Title: _____

_____

_____

_____

_____

_____

_____

_____

_____

_____

_____

_____

_____

_____

0-7424-1804-9 *Building Grammar & Writing Skills*

Name _____ Date _____

Out of This World

A **fantasy** is a story that could never happen. It contains events, ideas, or even imaginary worlds that do not and cannot exist. A fantasy story often contains magical aspects or journeys, quests, or dreams. Characters may include elves, fairies, leprechauns, wizards, giants, or talking animals or furniture.

You just found out that your chair can fly! Make notes on this page to help plan your fantasy story. Use your imagination! Write your story on another paper.

Beginning

Introduce the Main Characters (What do they look like? How do they act?)

Describe the Setting (house, school, castle, library, outer space, time of day, weather)

Hint at a Problem

Middle

Create Dialogue Between Characters
Show Characters' Actions
Hint at a Solution to the Problem

Show the Problem
Show Characters' Feelings

End

Show the Solution to the Problem

Show Characters' Feelings

117

Name _____ Date _____

Case of the Missing Cat

Finish writing this mystery.

Peter Radcliffe, my best friend, lived in a small brown and tan bungalow on the south side of Boxerville, just on the other side of the railroad tracks. Being an only child, he found a friend in his pet cat, Corona. Corona was a large, striped tabby that Peter got as a gift when he was two years old. Peter and Corona did everything together. The two were inseparable. The only time they were apart was when Peter had to go to school. However, Corona would lie on the front porch and not move until Peter came home.

One day, when Peter came home from school, Corona was not on the porch. He searched the house and the neighborhood, calling for him. "Where could he be?" Peter cried. "He never leaves the porch. I have to find him. It's getting colder at night, and Corona has never been out alone!" Peter needed help, so he ran to the phone and called me. Peter knew I was good at solving mysteries and could help him find Corona.

0-7424-1804-9 *Building Grammar & Writing Skills*

Name _____ Date _____

My Monster

Draw a picture of a monster in the box below. Give your monster a name. Write a description of your monster so a reader can actually visualize it in his or her mind. Use your five senses, including touch *(What does your monster's skin or fur feel like? Is it soft, prickly, rough?)*, sound *(What kinds of sounds does your monster make?)*, sight *(What does your monster look like? Is it big, small, hairy, colorful?)*, and smell *(Does your monster have a smell? Maybe it breathes fire and smells like burning coals.)*.

_____

_____

_____

_____

_____

0-7424-1804-9 *Building Grammar & Writing Skills*

Name _____ Date _____

Poetry in Motion

A **cinquain** is a five-line poem that has a specific number of words or syllables.

Line 1: The subject—one word or two syllables
Line 2: Adjectives—two words or four syllables
Line 3: Action verbs—three words or six syllables
Line 4: Descriptive phrase—four to five words or eight syllables
Line 5: Synonym or word that sums up the subject—one word or two syllables

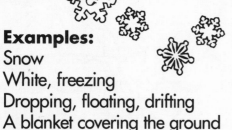

Examples:

Snow
White, freezing
Dropping, floating, drifting
A blanket covering the ground
Blizzard

Sneakers
Fluffy, speckled
Purring soft melodies
A special friend for everyone
Cat

Think about your favorite school subject, sport, animal, toy, or food. Brainstorm a list of words or phrases that describe this object or animal. You may use a thesaurus to find synonyms for this word. On a separate sheet of paper, write a cinquain. Draw a picture to accompany your poem.

120

Name _____ Date _____

Fabulous Friends

Alliteration is the repetition of an initial sound, usually of a consonant or cluster in two or more words in a line of poetry.

Fabulous Friends
Kristy's cooking casseroles,
While Freddie's frying fries.
Bubba's blowing bubbles,
While Darbi dances by.
Lilly's licking lollipops,
While Mindy makes money.
Sonja's sewing sweaters,
While Greg goes golfing.
Tom's tapping a tambourine
While Jenna does a jig.
These are my unique friends,
And I wouldn't trade them for anything!

Write your own alliteration poem about your friends or family members. First, list every person's name. Then list words that begin with the same letter or sound. On a separate sheet of paper, use these words to write a sentence about each person.

0-7424-1804-9 *Building Grammar & Writing Skills*

Name _____ Date _____

Fun with Limericks

A **limerick** is a humorous poem. It has five lines that consist of 13 beats. Lines 1, 2, and 5 have three beats and rhyme. Lines 3 and 4 have two beats and rhyme. The first line often begins with "There was a . . ." and ends with the name of a person or place. The last line ends with an unusual or outrageous rhyme.

There was a hairy man named Freddie
Who was so exceedingly sweaty,
When he ran
He was covered in sand
And looked like a sugar-coated teddy!

Before writing a limerick, make a list of places and names. Then list words that rhyme with these words. Finish your limerick with a funny rhyme. Use these frames to write your own limericks.

There once was a _____ from _____.
Who _____.
She/He asked _____.
Who/What/Where/When/Why/Will/Can _____.
And _____.

I once knew a _____ named _____.
All her/his/its life _____.
She/He/It _____.
And _____.
But _____.

0-7424-1804-9 *Building Grammar & Writing Skills*

Answer Key

Rollicking Riddles (Page 9)
1. Irene, Thompson, White, Avenue, Seattle, Aunt Diane, Rob, Aquarium, Gina, Oscar, Neptune, Father, Lexus, Yeager
   Riddle: It was a dragonfly.
2. Art, Jones, Indianapolis, Grandma, South, Academy, Winchel's
   Riddle: A jigsaw
3. Aunt, Carolyn, Oliver, Michigan, Building Riddle: A comb
4. Alice, Henry, Oscar, Lake, Erie
   Riddle: A hole

A Little Respect (Page 10)
1–4. Answers will vary.
5. Mr., Daniels
6. I, Dr., Williams
7. I, Senator, Harrison
8. Miss, Stanley, Mr., Parker, Ms., Cao
9. I, I
10. Professor, Pinedo
11. Sergeant, Davis, Captain, Riley
12. Mr., I, Judge, Yoshi

Capital Chaos (Page 11)
family, car, aunt, uncle's, beach, sister, bikes, father, pathway, dolphins, ocean, sandcastles, volleyball, hotel, swimming, mammoths, saber-toothed, mom, gift, sister, airport, vacation

Around the World (Page 12)
Paris, France   Montreal, Canada
Perth, Australia   Denver, Colorado
La Paz, Mexico   Ankara, Turkey
Beijing, China   Nairobi, Kenya
1. Rica, Central, America
2. Africa, Australia, Eastern
3. United, States
4. West, Illinois, Midwest
5. Japan, Hong, Kong, East
6. Jose, California, San, Francisco

Silly Scramble (Page 13)
1. Sunday
2. November, Thanksgiving
3. spring
4. Christmas, December
5. May, Mayo
6. autumn
7. Monday, Memorial Day
8. winter
9. Wednesday
10. July
11. summer
12. Columbus Day

Our Multilingual Nation (Page 14)
Hispanic, Italian, French, Mandarin, Chinese, Cantonese, Wu, Filipino, Tagalog, English, Spanish, German, Navajo, Hebrew

Tricky Titles (Page 15)
1. Harry Potter and the Chamber of Secrets
2. Coyotes in the Crosswalk
3. Amber Brown Is Not a Crayon
4. Kermit Takes the Walk
5. Red Wings Win in Overtime
6. Mario and Britney Play for Tennis Fans
7. Old Woman
8. The Old Guitarist
9. Young Bather with Sand Shovel
10–12. Answers will vary.

Camp Cayuga (Page 16)
August, Dear, Sonja, I, Camp, Cayuga, Pocono, Mountains, Northeast, Pennsylvania, They, You, Saturday, Appalachian, Trail, Sandy, Tina's, Dorney, Park, Wild, Kingdom, Hercules, Hercules, Hershey's, Chocolate, World, Amusement, Park, We, Hershey, Chocolate, I, Your, Maria

Crazy Quotes (Page 17)
1. Yes	2. Yes	3. No
4. No	5. No	6. Yes
7. No	8. No	9. Yes
10. Yes	11. No	12. No
13. No	14. Yes	15. Yes

Abbreviation Match-up (Page 18)
a.m.; A.M. — ante meridiem
in. — inches
etc. — et cetera
Aug. — August
Blvd. — Boulevard
cm — centimeter
Dec. — December
E. — East
Dr. — Doctor
Mrs. — Missus
Co. — Company
p.m.; P.M. — post meridiem

Feb. — February
Jr. — Junior
Mt. — Mountain; Mount
Oct. — October
Mr. — Mister
Gov. — Governor
misc. — miscellaneous
Fri. — Friday
Jan. — January
Gen. — General
ft. — foot; feet

kg — kilogram
ml — milliliter
oz. — ounce; ounces
qt. — quart; quarts
L — liter
yd. — yard
lb. — pound; pounds
p.; pp. — page; pages
no. — number

W. — West
vs.; v. — versus
Pres. — President
Sen. — Senator
Rev. — Reverend
Rep. — Representative
St. — Saint; Street
Sr. — Senior; Sister
Sept. — September
Wed. — Wednesday

Perfect Punctuation (Page 19)
1. .	2. ?	3. ?
4. .	5. .	6. !
7. .	8. ?	9. .
10. .	11. !	12. ?
13. !	14. .	15. .

Thank-You Letters (Page 20)
July 20, 2002
Dear Aunt Marilyn,
Your niece,

March 10, 2002
Toledo, OH 43617
Dear Mr. Broome:
Sincerely yours,

January 15, 2003
Anywhere, CA 90045
Dear Ms. Foster:
Sincerely,

December 5, 2002
Dear Ricky,
Love,

Tongue Twisters (Page 21)
1. Wendy, Wesley, and …
2. …steeple, sipping soda, sewing shirts, and ….
3. …Lannie, Lily, and …. lemons, licorice, and ….
4. Big Bill Boone, Bonnie Bell, and …
5. … hammock, played the harmonica, and …
6. Jonathan, Julie, Jacob, and …
7. … mini muffins, milks cows, and …
8–10. Answers will vary.

Comma Cleanup (Page 22)
1. …United States, Nathan?
   Oh, that's an easy …
2. Class, what …
   Yes, Stacey, do you …
   Yes, Mr. Davidson, Congress …
3. Jessica or Joaquin, could …
   Wow, that's a hard one!
   Mr. Davidson, I think I know.
   Yes, Joaquin.
   Very good, Joaquin.
4. Heather, what does …
   Hmmm, let me …
   Excellent job, Heather.
   Thank you, Mr. Davidson.

Published by Instructional Fair. Copyright protected.

0-7424-1804-9 *Building Grammar & Writing Skills*

Meet the Authors (Page 23)
1. .... Maniac Magee, the sixth ...
2. E.L. Konigsburg, the author ... Basil E. Frankweiler, grew up ...
3. ...Steve Crandell, a talented hockey player, who is ...
4. J.K. Rowling, author of the Harry Potter books, wrote ...
5. In 1969, Judy Blume published her first book, The One in ...
6. ...their dog, Chester.
7. Gary Soto, an acclaimed poet, essayist, and fiction writer, originally ... become a paleontologist, a scientist ...
8. Paula Danziger, a children's author of more than 25 books, knew ...

Cool Commas (Page 24)
1. I went to the store, and John went to the movies.
2. Mary ran to the car, but Bill ran to the bus.
3. It was raining all day, yet I was dry under my umbrella.
4. Vanessa ate the pizza, so Gillian ate the chocolate cake.
5. The puppy slept, and the cat played with a ball of yarn.
6. We played volleyball, for the weather was sunny and warm.
7. Kimberly will go to the grocery store, so she will not take a nap.
8. Mehrad will play baseball, or he will play football.
9. Kangaroos are furry, and they have a pocket.
10. Whales live in water, but they are not fish.

What Do You Say? (Page 25)
1. Logan asked, "May I get a dog for my birthday?"
2. "No, you're too young to have a dog," Mom replied.
3. "But, I am going to be five years old in December," whined Logan.
4. Mom explained, "Having a dog is...up after it."
5. Logan exclaimed, "I can do all ... care of it."
6. Jacob inquired, "What's Logan whining about?"
7. "He wants a ... he is too young," explained Mom.
8. Jacob commented, "I have always ... aren't I?"
9. Mom responded, "No, you may not get a dog."
10. "But, Mom, ... every day," Jacob explained.
11. ... said, "No, Jacob ... room."
12. ... together, "Can we ... year?"

Short Titles (Page 26)
1. "Gold Coin Rakes in Millions"
2. "Dangerous Floods in Europe"
3. "Spotlight on Kids' Safety"
4. "Justin's Music 101"
5–8. Answers will vary.

Titles Galore (Page 27)
1. Full Moon
2. How to Eat Fried Worms
3. The Phantom of the Opera
4. Courage the Cowardly Dog
5. Stuart Little 2
6. Full Sunlight, Rouen Cathedral
7–10. Answers will vary.

Pick the Possessive (Page 28)
1. My two brothers' bikes
2. The people's umbrellas
3. Each puppy's toys
4. Each boss's desk
5. My oldest grandfather's cars
6. The women's purses
7. An artist's brushes
8. My three sisters' room
9. That puppy's dish
10. The men's jackets
11. Rabbit's house
12. Matt's guitar

Marco Polo (Page 29)

m̲	Capitalize	(6 errors)
M̸	Lowercase	(3 errors)
⊙	Insert period	(3 errors)
∧	Insert comma	(8 errors)
∀	Insert apostrophe	(2 errors)
____	Underline	(1 error)

Parts of Speech Puzzle (Page 30)

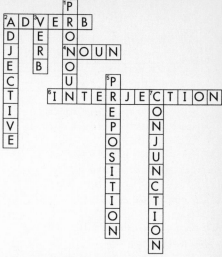

Recipe for Plurals (Page 31)
1. Add s—stereos, houses, friends, dinners, valleys
2. Add es—brushes, matches, glasses, tomatoes, boxes
3. Change y to i, add es—cities, babies, libraries, copies, groceries
4. Change f or fe to v, add es—loaves, calves, wives, knives, shelves
5. Irregular plurals—children, teeth, mice, feet, deer

Possessives Sort (Page 32)
1. more than one
2. one
3. more than one
4. one
5. one
6. one
7. one
8. more than one
9. more than one
10. more than one
11. one
12. more than one
13. one
14. more than one
15. more than one

Marco Polo was born in venice in 1254. He was an italian merchant and explorer. He was the first european to cross the entire continent of Asia and leave a record of what he saw and heard.

Marco Polo's father Nicolo Polo was a merchant Nicolo and his brother left on a trading mission to China when Marco was only six years old. Marco was 15 years old by the time his father and uncle returned to Venice. His Mother had died while his father was away and his Aunt and uncle raised him. When he was 17, he accompanied his Father and uncle on a journey to china, traveling along the Silk road and reaching the court of Kublai Khan. He served as a government official to Kublai Khan. Their travels took them all over Asia.

The Polos returned to Venice in 1295. They had been gone for 24 years. They brought back many riches—ivory jade jewels, porcelain, silk, and other treasures. However, when they returned, Venice was at war with Genoa In 1296, Marco Polo, a captain of the Venetian galley was captured. While jailed, he dictated to a fellow prisoner what he saw and heard while he traveled. Marco Polo's book The Travels of Marco Polo was one of the most popular books in medieval Europe. Marco Polo died in 1324 when he was 70 years old.

0-7424-1804-9 *Building Grammar & Writing Skills*

Birthday Party (Page 33)

1. She
2. They
3. He
4. She
5. They
6. them
7. We
8. it
9. We
10. her
11. we
12. him
13. she

Pronoun Power (Page 34)

1. he
2. She
3. They, her
4. We, them, them, her
5. us, O
6. It, S
7. him, O
8. he, S

It's a Cover-up (Page 35)

His—William's room is messy.
Her—Allison's car is fast.
Hers—That balloon is Heather's.
Our—Callie's and my bedroom is clean.
Ours—The ball is Philip's and mine.
Their—The Sessler's house is big.
Theirs—This boat is the Harrison's.
Its—The elephant's trunk is long.
Her—Mrs. Smith's hair is brown.
Hers—These glasses are Miss Henry's.
His—Mr. Krug's bike needs repairs.
His—That is Tad's football.

In the Past (Page 36)

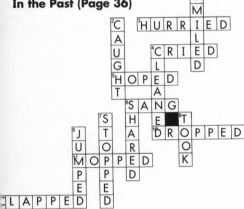

Go Fish! Verbs Game (Page 37)

broken	bring	caught
chosen	come	drank
driven	fly	gave
gone	grow	hid
known	ride	rang
seen	sing	spoke
swum	take	threw
written		

A Little Help (Page 38)

1. has visited
2. is planning
3. will raise
4. have planned
5. will give
6. has played
7. are selling
8. are collecting
9. have donated
10. am writing
11. are making
12. shall post

A Tall Tale (Page 39)

1. is
2. were
3. was
4. were
5. was
6. was
7. were
8. were
9. been
10. being
11. was
12. be

Lots of Links (Page 40)

1. New York is a city.
2. Jason appeared happy when he won the race.
3. The fourth graders are very excited for the field trip.
4. The spaghetti tastes delicious.
5. Everybody stayed calm when the fire alarm went off.
6. Victor sounded very surprised when he won the writing contest.
7. The best swimmers were Margie and Cathie.
8. Elizabeth seems happy to be back home.
9. Grandma looks really tired.
10. Mehrad's brother became a doctor.
11. The monkey looked hungry.
12. I am excited because tomorrow is my birthday!

Describing Details (Page 41)

Answers will vary.

Let's Compare (Page 42)

Answers will vary.

Assorted Adverbs (Page 43)

How

She sings beautifully.
Hector talked quietly to his sister.
The cat crept slowly to the fence.
I carefully washed the expensive vase.
Stacey can clearly see the road signs.
The water flowed rapidly.
Cassie scratched Rover's ear softly.
We cheered happily when she won.
Jenna laughed loudly at the funny clown.

Where

The party will take place here.
Put the box there, on the table.
The lake was nearby.
We will meet here after the movie.
I left my gloves somewhere.
Let's go home.
Jeremy happed over the puddle.
I want to go over to that museum.
The clever fox hid behind the tree.

When

Now it's time to open the presents!
Today we will visit our grandparents.
Erin's story will be published later.
Emily often orders plain spaghetti.
I'll check out of the hotel tomorrow.
It was too soon to tell.
Pam will know the answer soon.
Katie is always late to dance class.

Merely Modifying (Page 44)

Adverbs

Anita plays the piano beautifully.
Mr. Henderson dresses casually.
The microwave can cook food fast.
James walks quickly to school.
I am going to the circus tomorrow.

Adjectives

My grandparents have a small house.
The soup is very hot.
She is an intelligent woman.

Preposition Puzzle (Page 45)

1. around
2. underneath
3. into
4. without
5. across
6. for
7. under
8. inside
9. until
10. through
11. over
12. from
13. during
14. behind

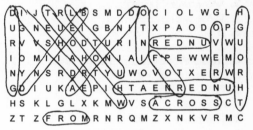

Conjunction Function (Page 46)

1. Words – and
2. Phrases – or
3. Clauses – but
4. Clauses – so
5. Clauses – for
6. Words – yet
7. Phrases – and
8. Phrases – or
9. Clauses – yet
10. Phrases – but
11. Words – or
12. Clauses – so
13. Words – and
14. Clauses – so

Awesome Interjections! (Page 47)

1. Hey!
2. Wow!
3. Oh yeah!
4. No way!
5. Hurry!
6. Oh dear!
7. Yikes!
8. Eeeeek!
9. Ah!
10. Whoa!
11. Whew!
12. Awesome!
13–15. Answers will vary.

The Plural Express (Page 48)

1. turkeys, geese
2. daisies, peaches
3. shelves, glasses
4. men, deer
5. peaks, valleys
6. children, universities
7. mice, fish
8. cities, museums
9. cows, calves
10. sisters, parties
11. boxes, bunches
12. bushes, dishes

0-7424-1804-9 *Building Grammar & Writing Skills*

It's Mine! (Page 49)

1. puppies
2. boy's
3. students'
4. shoes
5. Ladies'
6. clowns
7. women's
8. horses
9. girls'
10. dog's
11. Mom's
12. dolphins
13. classes'
14. turtle's

At the Movies (Page 50)

1. X Iggy and I ...
2. X She and I ...
3. X I like ...
4. X Iggy will sit ... Wiggy and him.
5. X Iggy told him ...
6. C
7. C
8. X He saw the ...
9. C
10. X Wiggy wants her to ...
11. C
12. X Wiggy and I didn't ...
13. X Wiggy often ... with me.
14. C

Confusing Words (Page 51)

1. You're
2. It's
3. Its
4. their
5. it's
6. you're
7. They're
8. your
9. your
10. their

Let's Agree (Page 52)

1. play
2. barks
3. make
4. practice
5. bake
6. stretch
7. chases
8. skates
9. walk
10. laugh
11. skip
12. catches

Write It Right (Page 53)

1. I went to my grandmother's house.
2. My sister broke my mom's watch.
3. I caught the ball.
4. My class read 145 books for the reading contest.
5. I was so thirsty that I drank the whole glass of water!
6. We swam in my aunt's pool all day.
7. Mom, Leslie took my dinosaur.
8. My grandpa taught me how to ride a bike.
9. Dad, Bill threw the baseball right through that window!
10. Emily brought her baseball cards to school for show-and-tell.
11. My little sister drew all over my science project.
12. She tore my math homework in half, too.

Talent Show (Page 54)

1. correct
2. come
3. correct
4. gave
5. sang
6. written
7. correct
8. correct
9. knew
10. correct
11. did
12. gone
13. correct
14. forgot
15. get

A Monster Challenge (Page 55)

1. lie
2. Lay
3. lay
4. lie
5. lies
6. lays
7. lies
8. lays
9. lies
10. Lay
11. lie
12. lays

Read-a-Thon (Page 56)

1. is
2. have
3. is
4. is
5. is
6. had
7. were
8. had, had
9. did
10. had
11. has
12. has

Adjective Wise (Page 57)

1. hardest
2. funniest
3. closer
4. more colorful
5. brightest
6. most delicious
7. more interesting
8. longer
9. most confusing
10. more graceful
11. sweeter
12. most embarrassing

Adverb Adventure (Page 58)

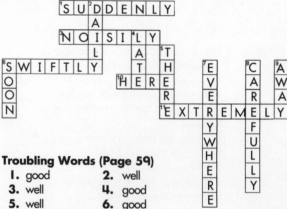

Troubling Words (Page 59)

1. good
2. well
3. well
4. good
5. well
6. good
7. well
8. good
9. well
10. good
11. well
12. good
13. well
14. well

Peppy Prepositions (Page 60)

Where's the Animal? (Page 61)

Sample Answers:

1. The goat is on top of the umbrella.
2. A fox is inside the box.
3. An elephant is under the table.
4. The giraffes are in front of the tree.
5. A cat is jumping over the hat.
6. The rabbit is hopping over the chair.

Let's Connect (Page 62)

1. Renee and Michel like pudding for dessert.
2. Kim and Nicholas are leaving on Friday.
3. Jose or Rebecca will answer the question.
4. Randy, Sean, and/or Rudy will make cookies.
5. The day was sunny and warm.
6. Tina will play hopscotch and/or tag.
7. Freddie washed and waxed his car.

0-7424-1804-9 *Building Grammar & Writing Skills*

My Topic and Purpose (Page 64)

Purpose: to entertain
Audience: classmates and teachers — Why does a dog make a good pet?

Purpose: to talk someone into something (persuade)
Audience: voters — Support me for president

Purpose: to give information
Audience: skateboarders — What are the advantages and disadvantages to wearing a helmet?

Purpose: to talk someone into something (persuade)
Audience: mom and dad — How to get good grades

Purpose: to provide information
Audience: science fair judges — How a liquid changes into a gas

Purpose: to explain
Audience: chefs — How to make an apple pie

Purpose: to give information
Audience: little brother — What if you found a dinosaur in your backyard?

Writing Styles (Page 65)

1. Expository
2. Persuasive
3. Expository
4. Narrative
5. Descriptive
6. Persuasive
7. Descriptive
8. Narrative

Graphic Organizers (Page 66)

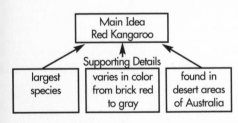

Organize Your Outline (Page 67)

1. I. Flowers, II. Trees
2. I. Fruit, II. Vegetables
3. I. Fish, II. Shellfish
4. I. Birds, II. Insects
5. I. Farm Animals, II. Zoo Animals

Many Musical Instruments (Page 68)

The Order May Vary:
  I. Percussion Instruments
    A. Kettledrum   B. Bass drum
    C. Snare drum   D. Cymbals
  II. Brass Instruments
    A. Trombone   B. Trumpet
    C. French horn   D. Bugle
  III. Stringed Instruments
    A. Violin   B. Harp
    C. Cello   D. Bass
  IV. Woodwind Instruments
    A. Clarinet   B. Flute
    C. Saxophone   D. Piccolo
  V. Keyboard Instruments
    A. Piano   B. Organ
    C. Harpsichord

What Is It? (Page 69)

Possible Answers:
Title: Differences Between a Yam and Sweet Potato
  I. Yam and Sweet Potato
    A. Plant families differ
    B. Eat different parts of the plant
    C. Appearance
    D. Taste
    E. Where they are grown

Details, Details (Page 70)

  I. Plants
    A1. Pine, A2. Maple
    B1. Rose, B2. Petunia
  II. Animals
    A1. Whale, A2. Bear
    B1. Seagull, B2. Robin
  I. Winter
    A1. Cold, A2. Snowy
    B1. Ice skating, B2. Sledding
  II. Summer
    A1. Sunny, A2 .Hot
    B1. Water skiing, B2. Swimming

Wild Kingdom (Page 71)

The Order May Vary:
  I. Vertebrates
    A. Mammals
    A1. Giraffes   A2. Foxes
    B. Reptiles
    B1. Crocodiles
    B2. Alligators
    C. Amphibians
    C1. Frogs
    C2. Salamanders
  II. Invertebrates
    A. Insects
    A1. Ants
    A2. Dragonflies
    A3. Butterflies
    B. Jellyfish
    C. Spiders

What's the Point? (Page 72)

Answers will vary.

Terrific Topics (Page 73)

Answers will vary.

In Harmony (Page 74)

1. Topic Sentence: Owning a pet is a major responsibility.
   Unrelated Sentence: I had a pet hamster, but it died.
2. Topic Sentence: No matter what mascot wins, an election is a special and exciting occasion.
   Unrelated Sentence: On Saturday, I am going to watch our school football team play the Tigers.
3. Topic Sentence: My Dad and I are throwing a surprise birthday party for her.
   Unrelated Sentence: Last year, we took my mom out to eat for her birthday.
4. Topic Sentence: The library is one of my favorite places in the world.
   Unrelated Sentence: My favorite author is Matt Christopher.

Make It Flow (Page 75)

Possible Answers:
1. I use to be an only child until my parents had my two brothers. Now my life is chaos, because my brothers constantly run around, yell, scream, and get into trouble.
2. My older brother, Jacob, constantly teases me. My younger brother, Logan, always uses my crayons without my permission and breaks them. However, I love them both.
3. Floppy, our rabbit, escaped from her pen. When we tried to catch her, she hopped away from us. Consequently, we had to try something else. I dangled a carrot to get her attention. Meanwhile, my brother sneaked up behind her. However, the moment he was about to grab her, she hopped away. As a result, my brother landed flat on his face.

Silly Sequences (Page 76)

1. 4, 3, 6, 1, 5, 2
2. 2, 3, 1

Cats and Dogs (Page 77)

Possible Answers:
Alike—4 legs, 2 eyes, 2 ears, tail, fur
Different—Cats are independent, dogs are not. Cats meow, dogs bark. Cats don't like water.

0-7424-1804-9 *Building Grammar & Writing Skills*

Wrapping It Up (Page 78)
Possible Answers:
1. I wish every day could be my birthday.
2. Have you ever seen "Old Man River"?
3. Owls are birds of the night.
4. Do you hold and pet your puppy?

A Perfect Paragraph (Page 79)
Answers will vary.

What an Introduction! (Page 81)
Answers will vary.

Outlaw Run-ons (Page 82)
1. playground. Still,   2. chooses. They
3. plans. We   4. up. Therefore,
5. consider. It   6. tomorrow. I
7. me. I   8. alone. They
9. yesterday. I . . . nesting. Look
10. sun. Try

Easy Elaboration (Page 83)
Answers will vary.

Good Choices (Page 84)
Possible Answers:
1. delicious   2. bawled
3. scurried   4. inquired
5. jogged   6. in disarray
7. tragedy   8. bolted
9. elated   10. beautiful

Sly as a Fox (Page 85)
Possible Answers:
1. a horse   2. an apple
3. a penguin   4. a car
5. buffaloes   6. an ox
7. a cheetah   8. leather
9. marshmallows
Possible Answers:
10–14. Answers will vary.

He's a Monster (Page 86)
1. a fierce shark   2. a wall
3. a balloon   4. explosive volcanoes
5. a thick blanket   6. a bolt of lightning
8–10. Answers will vary.

It's All in the Almanac (Page 87)
1. Page 481
2. Postal Information
3. United States Populations
4. Page 576
5. Sports
6. Awards, Medals, Prizes; page 316
7. United States Cities
8. Presidential Elections

Amazing Almanac (Page 88)
Answers will vary.

Guide Words (Page 89)
1. ear pick   • eastern
2. bulletin   • buncos
3. luminaria   • lupus erthernatosus
4. off-the-books   • old
5. platonic   • player
6. disgraceful   • disinterestedly
7. systematic   • tableful
8. campylobacter   • candidature
9. applicative   • approved

Encyclopedia Search (Page 90)
1. birds – Volume 2 B
2. Vikings – Volume 20 U–V
3. cardinal – Volume 3 C–Ch
4. solar system – Volume 18 So–Sz
5. cello – Volume 3 C–Ch
6. Henry Ford – Volume 7 F
7. constellation – Volume 4 Ci–Cz
8. silverfish – Volume 17 S–Sn
9. black widow – Volume 2 B
10. jack rabbit – Volume 16 Q–R
11. Emily Dickinson – Volume 5 D
12. U.S. Government – Volume 20 U–V
13. spiders – Volume 18 So–Sz
14. Johnny Appleseed – Volume 1 A
15. Olympic Games – Volume 14 N–O
16. San Diego – Volume 17 S–Sn
17. gorilla – Volume 8 G
18. Mars – Volume 13 M
19. xylophone – Volume 21 W–Z
20. George Washington – Volume 21 W–Z
21. racquetball – Volume 16 Q–R
22. Revolutionary War – Volume 16 Q–R

At the Library (Page 91)
Title: The World of the Spider
Author: Adrianna Mason
Publisher: Sierra Club Books
Call No.: 595.44
Copyright Date: 1999
Illustrator: Kimberly Smith
Summary: Examines the physical characteristics, behavior, and habitats of different kinds of spiders.
No. of Pages: 116

Show Me (Page 92)
Answers will vary.

Taking Notes (Page 93)
Possible Answers:
The U.S. Constitution creates three branches of government.
1. Congress – legislative branch – Senate and House of Representatives, makes laws, declares war, collects and spends tax money.
2. Executive branch – enforces the laws; president, vice president, and cabinet members; president is head; appoints cabinet members; signs and enforces laws; serves as head of the armed forces; makes treaties; cabinet members advise president.
3. Judicial branch – federal courts, judges, interprets our laws, Supreme Court is the highest court.

0-7424-1804-9 *Building Grammar & Writing Skills*